高橋和希

I BELIEVE THAT EVERYONE HAS AN "OTHER SELF" INSIDE THEM. IT MAY BE YOUR IDEAL SELF, SOMEONE WHO IT'S YOUR GOAL TO BECOME. BUT WHEN YOU'RE PRESSURED TO BE A CERTAIN WAY BY THE EXPECTATIONS OF YOUR PARENTS OR THE WORLD, THE BURDEN MAY BE TOO MUCH TO BEAR, AND YOU MAY LOSE SIGHT OF YOURSELF. IN OTHER WORDS, YOUR "OTHER SELF" IS SOMETHING YOU YOURSELF HAVE TO CREATE, NOT THAT OTHER PEOPLE CAN FORCE UPON YOU. I THINK IT'S BEST TO TAKE IT EASY, KEEP AN EYE ON YOUR "OTHER SELF," AND AIM FOR THAT GOAL...BUT DON'T STRESS OUT ABOUT REACHING IT RIGHT AWAY.

—KAZUKI TAKAHASHI, 1998

Artist/author Kazuki Takahashi first tried to break into the manga business in 1982, but success eluded him until **Yu-Gi-Oh!** debuted in the Japanese **Weekly Shonen Jump** magazine in 1996. **Yu-Gi-Oh!**'s themes of friendship and fighting, together with Takahashi's weird and wonderful art, soon became enormously successful, spawning a real-world card game, video games, and two anime series. A lifelong gamer, Takahashi enjoys Shogi (Japanese chess), Mahjong, card games, and tabletop RPGs, among other games.

YU-GI-OH! DUELIST VOL. 2
Gollancz Manga Edition

STORY AND ART BY
KAZUKI TAKAHASHI

Translation & English Adaptation/Joe Yamazaki
Touch-Up Art & Lettering/Rina Mapa
Design/Sean Lee
Editor/Jason Thompson
UK Cover Adaptation/Sue Michniewicz

YU-GI-OH! © 1996 by Kazuki Takahashi. All rights reserved. First published
in Japan in 1996 by SHUEISHA Inc., Tokyo. English publication rights in the
United Kingdom arranged by SHUEISHA Inc. through VIZ Media, LLC, U.S.A.,
Tuttle-Mori Agency, Inc., Japan and Ed Victor Ltd., U.K. This edition
published in Great Britain in 2006 by Gollancz Manga, an imprint of the
Orion Publishing Group, Orion House, 5 Upper St Martin's Lane, London
WC2H 9EA, and a licensee of VIZ Media, LLC.

1 3 5 7 9 10 8 6 4 2

The right of Kazuki Takahashi to be identified as the
author of this work has been asserted by him in accordance
with the Copyright, Designs and Patents Act 1988.

A CIP catalogue record for this book is available from the British Library

ISBN 0 57507 759 X
ISBN 9 780 57507 759 1

Printed and bound at Mackays of Chatham, PLC

PARENTAL ADVISORY
Yu-Gi-Oh! is rated "T" for teens. It may contain violence,
language, alcohol or tobacco usage, or suggestive situations.
It is recommended for ages 13 and up.

The Orion Publishing Group's policy is to use papers that
are natural, renewable and recyclable products and made from
wood grown in sustainable forests. The logging and manufacturing
processes are expected to conform to the environmental
regulations of the country of origin.

SHONEN JUMP

www.orionbooks.co.uk

SHONEN JUMP GRAPHIC NOVEL

Vol. 2
THE PUPPET MASTER

STORY AND ART BY
KAZUKI TAKAHASHI

⟨MAIN CAST⟩

THE STORY SO FAR...

When 10th grader Yugi solved the Millennium Puzzle, he became Yu-Gi-Oh, the King of Games, a dark avenger who challenged evildoers to "Shadow Games" of life and death. But Yugi isn't the only gamer with a strange powers. Maximillion Pegasus, creator of the world's No. 1 collectible card game, challenged Yugi to enter a "Duel Monsters" tournament on his private island, Duelist Kingdom. Can Yugi and Jonouchi fight their way through dozens of duelists to win the grand prize...and discover the secret of the Millennium Items?

武藤遊戯
YUGI MUTOU/DARK YUGI

The main character.

When he solved the ancient Egyptian Millennium Puzzle, he developed an alter ego, the King of Games, which emerges in times of stress.

城之内克也
KATSUYA JONOUCHI

Yugi's classmate, a tough guy who's still a novice at "Duel Monsters." He wants to use the tournament prize money to pay for his sister's eye surgery. In the English anime he's known as "Joey Wheeler."

武藤双六
SUGOROKU MUTOU

Yugi's grandfather, the owner of the Kame ("Turtle") game store. To force Yugi to enter his tournament, Pegasus imprisoned Sugoroku's soul inside a videotape, leaving his body in a coma.

本田ヒロト
HIROTO HONDA

Yugi's classmate, a friend of Jonouchi. In the English anime he's known as "Tristan Taylor."

真崎杏子
ANZU MAZAKI

Yugi's classmate and childhood friend. Her first name means "Peach." In the English anime she's known as "Téa Gardner."

獏良 了
RYO BAKURA

Like Yugi and Pegasus, Bakura owns a Millennium Item: the Millennium Ring. Unfortunately for him, it's possessed by an evil spirit.

ペガサス・J・クロフォード
MAXIMILLION J. PEGASUS

The American game designer who created "Duel Monsters." His Millennium Eye gives him the power to read people's minds. In the original Japanese manga he's called "Pegasus J. Crawford."

Vol. 2

CONTENTS

OH NO...!

FsssSS

HARPY LADY ★★★★★

ATK/1300
DEF/1400

HARPY LADY
Attack Power
Boosted by
Mountains
1690

HARPY LADY NO. 1!

SLASH

NO *NEWBIE* CAN BEAT ME, *LITTLE BOY!*

HEH HEH...

KILL "TIGER AXE"!

DUEL 11: THINGS THAT DON'T CHANGE

YOU CAN STILL WIN!

DON'T PANIC, JONOUCHI!

AWW, MAN...! IS THERE *ANY* WAY JONOUCHI CAN WIN...?!

JONOUCHI!

DUEL 11: THINGS THAT DON'T CHANGE

LASH

OHO HO HO HO! PRE-PARE TO DIE!!

LASH

THE DEMON HUNTER IS DES-TROYED!

UG-YAA!

ELECTRO-WHIP

HARPY LADY'S ATTACK GOES UP 300 POINTS!

HARPY LADY
Attack
1990

WELL TAKE THIS!

OH YEAH?!

WARRIOR OF GARDNA!

YOU WON'T BE ABLE TO BEAT MY HARPY LADY WITH A CARD LIKE THAT!

EACH TURN, SHE BECOMES MORE BEAUTIFUL... MORE ELEGANT... AND MOST OF ALL, STRONGER

HEH HEH...

AGAIN... SHE KNEW WHAT CARD IT WAS BEFORE SHE TURNED IT OVER!

BBMP

FSSSH

JONOUCHI
Life Points 1120

I CAN'T BEAT HER...

I'M JUST NOT GOOD ENOUGH...

!

VSH

HEY, YOU OUT THERE!

...

C'MON, JONO-UCHI!

AND YOU'LL HELP HIM WIN...?

"IF YOU SHOUT, THE DUELIST WILL HEAR YOUR FEELINGS...?"

WHAT WAS IT YOU SAID...?

THAT KIND OF THING'S USELESS.

WELL?

DO YOU SEE NOW?

!!

HE NEEDS ALL THE "FEEL-INGS" YOU'VE GOT!

THEN MAKE THIS WIMP WIN!

...!

TODAY'S FRIENDS ARE TOMOR-ROW'S ENEMIES! THAT'S WHAT IT MEANS TO BE A DUELIST!

YOU CAN'T BECOME A TRUE DUELIST AND PLAY WITH YOUR FRIENDS AT THE SAME TIME!

AND HERE'S SOME MORE FREE ADVICE, BOY

HEH HEH...

SOME-
THING
YOU CAN
SHOW BUT
YOU CAN'T
SEE...?

!!

SOUNDS
GREAT!
I WANNA
SEE
THIS! I'M
WAITING!

YEAH,
THAT'S A
STRATEGY!
THAT'S
GOING TO
MAKE HIM
WIN, ALL
RIGHT!

AHA
HA
HA
HA
HA!

...

BUT...
THIS TIME
NOT EVEN
THAT CAN
MAKE ME
WIN...

C'MON...
IT'S
FRIEND-
SHIP!

THANKS
FOR
SHOWING
ME THAT
WE'RE
FRIENDS.

YOU
GIVE
UP!

YUGI
...

I
KNOW
THE
ANSWER
TO
THAT...

SHIZUKA...
I WISH YOU
WERE
HERE...
I WISH
I COULD
SEE YOU...

I DON'T
KNOW WHAT
YOU'RE
TRYING
TO TELL
ME...

I'M
SORRY,
YUGI...

...

...

I'M
TOO
DUMB
TO FIGURE
OUT
WHAT YOU
MEAN...

I CAN'T EVEN FIX YOUR EYES...

I'M A ROTTEN BROTHER...

OH, SHIZUKA...

FOR ONE LAST TIME...

I WANTED TO SEE YOUR FACE...

CRAP!

...

HUH...?

I CAN'T LET YOU GO TO THAT KIND OF WORLD...!

SHIZUKA...

THE WORLD OF BLINDNESS... I WONDER IF IT'S PITCH BLACK LIKE THIS...

I NOTICED FOR THE FIRST TIME WHEN MY EYES WERE CLOSED! BUT, WHY...?

...I CAN SMELL LOTS OF DIFFERENT PERFUMES! THEY'RE EACH DISTINCT!

I DIDN'T REALIZE AT ALL WHEN MY EYES WERE OPEN...

I JUST THOUGHT IT WAS THE PERFUME SHE WAS WEARING... BUT...

WHAT IS THIS...?

I SMELL SOMETHING...

C'MON! IT'S YOUR TURN! I HAVEN'T GOT ALL DAY!

...YOU'RE ABLE TO TELL WHICH CARDS ARE IN YOUR HAND BY SMELLING THEM!

BY PUTTING DIFFERENT PERFUMES ON ALL THE CARDS IN ADVANCE...

WHAT!?

I GET IT! I KNOW YOUR CARD TRICK!

GASP

SOMETHING YOU CAN SHOW BUT CAN'T SEE!

BUT YOU CAN'T SEE THE SMELL...

YOU CAN SHOW THE CARDS...

BABY DRAGON

★★★★

ATK/1200
DEF/700

I PLAY THE BABY DRAGON!

HERE I COME!

B BMP

B am

BWP

DEFENSE MODE!

THAT CARD ...!

!

WELL, AT LEAST YOU WERE SMART ENOUGH TO PUT IT IN DEFENSE MODE, SO YOU WON'T GET HURT WHEN I KILL IT!

SO INSTEAD OF KILLING IT, I'LL PLAY THIS CARD!

GOOD CHOICE-- A CARD FOR BABIES!

AHA HA HA!

I'M NOT GONNA WASTE THE CARD YOU GAVE ME!

WATCH ME, YUGI!

I GAVE THAT CARD TO JONO-UCHI!

THAT'S THE HARPY LADIES' ELEGANT 10-HIT COMBO!

AHA HA HA HA!

IT'S LIKE I SAID! EVERY TURN THEY GET *STRONGER* AND MORE *BEAUTIFUL!*

I DON'T HAVE A CARD THAT CAN BEAT THREE HARPIES ...!

ULP ...

JONOUCHI
Life Points **120**

I CAN'T WIN...MY BACK'S AGAINST THE WALL ...!

...!

DON'T GIVE UP, JONOUCHI!

ASIDE FROM THE HARPY LADY, SHE HAS NO OTHER MONSTER CARDS IN HER DECK!

IF HER HARPY LADY DIES, HER WHOLE STRATEGY FALLS APART!

BUT BECAUSE IT'S THAT SIMPLE, IT HAS A CRITICAL WEAK-NESS!

NAME-LY...

MAI KUJAKU'S COMBO IS BASED ON POWERING-UP ONE HARPY LADY WITH MORE THAN 10 MAGIC CARDS AND EQUIPMENT CARDS!

THE TIME WIZARD!!

JONO-UCHI, TRUST THE CARDS!

RMMBB

I'LL HAVE TO DRAW IT...!

I ONLY HAVE ONE CHANCE...!

B-BUT I DON'T HAVE THE TIME WIZARD CARD IN MY HAND RIGHT NOW...

YOU'VE GOT ONE TURN TO LIVE!

C'MON!

WHY DON'T YOU JUST GIVE UP AND GIVE ME YOUR CARDS RIGHT NOW?

GGKK...

FLASH

PLEASE BE IT!

HERE GOES!

WP

TIME MAGIC !!

GO, TIME WIZARD !

DGOOM

BABY DRAGON, BECOME THE THOU- SAND DRAGON !

THOUSAND DRAGON
Attack
2400

HUH ...!?

SO WHAT!? THAT SENILE DRAGON IS NOTHING! MY HARPIES' ATTACK IS STRONGER!

HMPH !

KILL IT, HARPY LADY SISTERS !

M-MY HARPIES ARE WRINKLY... WITH GREY HAIR...!

BA BA

GROAN

HARPY LADY
Attack
1300

HARPY LADY
Attack
1300

HARPY LADY
Attack
1300

WH-WHAT--!?

GO. THOU-SAND DRAGON!!

ALL RIGHT!

I-I'M SUR-PRISED TOO...

I DIDN'T KNOW IT'D DO THAT...

WHOA--

POOR MAI KUJAKU... NOT ONLY LOSING, BUT LOSING YOUR BEAUTY, MAY HAVE BEEN TOO CRUEL...

HEH HEH... JUST AS I THOUGHT! 100 YEARS PASSED ON THE SPOT AND THE HARPY LADIES GREW OLD AND LOST THEIR POWERS!

THOU-SAND NOSE BREATH!!

AIEEE!

SIIIRRF

THANKS, YUGI!

JONO-UCHI WON!

YES! HE DID IT!

YAY

IT'S A MIRA-CLE---!

I...I LOST...

N-NOOO!

MAI KUJAKU
Life Points 0

SOME-THING YOU CAN SHOW...

...BUT YOU CAN'T SEE!

IT'S...

THERE'S ONE THING THAT DOESN'T CHANGE EVEN AFTER 100 YEARS...

WHAT...!?

MAI KUJAKU... I MAY NOT BE A "TRUE" DUELIST BUT LET ME TELL YOU THIS...

DUEL 12: THE SCOURGE OF THE SEA

Duelist Kingdom

4 HOURS HAVE PASSED SINCE THE TOURNAMENT BEGAN (44 HOURS REMAINING)

HEH HEH...

JONO-UCHI: TWO STAR CHIPS!

YUGI: THREE STAR CHIPS!

29

WE CAN'T NOT EAT OR DRINK FOR 48 HOURS!

THE GAME LASTS TWO WHOLE DAYS ...!

THAT'S A PROBLEM ...

HOW CHEAP! THAT LONG-HAIRED FOREIGNER ...

YOU'D THINK THE PERSON WHO BROUGHT US HERE WOULD FEED US!

WARNING! SEXIST COMMENT ALERT!

YOU'RE A GIRL! YOU'RE SUPPOSED TO MAKE LUNCH!

THIS IS YOUR FAULT, ANZU! WHY DIDN'T YOU THINK AHEAD?

WHAT'S THAT? SOMETHING SMELLS GOOD ...!

SNIFF SNIFF

?

HM ...?

N-NO WAY...! I'M NOT EATING NO MUSH-ROOMS --!

OH WELL! IF IT COMES DOWN TO IT, WE'LL USE THIS BOOK TO FIND OUT WHAT PLANTS AND MUSHROOMS WE CAN EAT!

Survival Book

JUST LIKE WHEN HE FOUGHT MAI KUJAKU... HIS SENSE OF SMELL IS LIKE A DOG'S...

WHAT SMELL ...?

TMP TMP

LET'S GO GUYS !!

IT'S COMING FROM THE OCEAN !!

STOP! THAT'S NOT YOURS!

JONOUCHI! YOU'RE NOT GONNA ...!

NOW'S OUR CHANCE!

NO-BODY'S HERE!

H-HE'S RIGHT!

I FOUND FOOD!

LOOK AT THAT!

GULP

I'M *NEVER* PLAYING A GAME WITH YOU...

OH BOY ...

I'M WITH JONO-UCHI!

YOU TOO?!

AU CONTRAIRE, ANZU! THE LAW OF THIS ISLAND IS, WHOEVER STEALS THE STAR CHIPS WINS!

SO STEALING FOOD'S *GOTTA* BE OKAY! IT'S ALL PART OF... *"THE GAME OF LIFE!"*

SIZZLE

gulp

LET'S DIG IN!

splash

MM ...!!

sh

IT SMELLS GREAT!

MAN, THAT LOOKS GOOD!

YOU ...

WHY ...

YOU ...

WHAT THE--?!?!

AT FIRST GLANCE, HE DOESN'T LOOK LIKE THE KIND OF GUY WHO PLAYS CARD GAMES...BUT I GUESS YOU NEVER KNOW...

RYOTA KAJIKI ...

DON'T THROW IT AWAY! WE CAN EAT IT--!!

SMALL FRY!

...

SNICKER ...

OCTO-PUS...

SO LET ME GET THIS STRAIGHT... YOU GUYS ARE...

AS I WAS SAYING... YOU GUYS ARE DUELISTS TOO, EH?

OUR OCTO-PUS --!

I MIGHT'VE JUST MADE A BIG CATCH!

GASP!

IT'S HIM! THAT GUY... YUGI!

HUH ...?

HEH ...

MMM! HEH HEH ...

THESE FISH ARE JUST ABOUT DONE!

NOW THEN ...

KRKL

...

LEAVE SOME FOR US!

SLURP MUNCH

AWW, THANKS, MAN!

YOU MEAN IT?

YOU GUYS CAN EAT TOO!

ALL RIGHT, ALL RIGHT!

HEH HEH!

YOU BET!

DID YOU ENTER THIS TOURNAMENT FOR THE PRIZE TOO?

SO, KAJIKI ...

I'M STUFFED!

PHEW ...!

THANK YOU SO MUCH!

WA HA HA HA

I'M GONNA GET THE LATEST SONAR EQUIPPED BOAT!!

I HEAR THE PRIZE IS *HUGE!*

I'LL GET A BIG CATCH *EVERY DAY!*

THEN I'LL BE ABLE TO FISH AGAIN!

I'M GONNA SPEND THE PRIZE MONEY ON A BOAT!

SHAA AA AA

THAT'S A COOL WAY TO LIVE!

A BOAT, HUH?

...I CAN TELL WHEN IT LAUGHS AND WHEN IT CRIES.

IT'S JUST LIKE A PERSON TO ME...

I GREW UP WATCHING THE SEA FROM THE DAY I WAS BORN.

BUT THEN...

ITS MOOD CHANGED...

THE OCEAN WAS IN A GOOD MOOD...

A COUPLE YEARS AGO I WAS OUT FISHING WITH MY DAD, LIKE USUAL...

BUT IT WORKS BOTH WAYS!

THE OCEAN WATCHES US TOO!

MY DAD AND I WERE SAVED BY A PASSING SHIP...WE WERE LUCKY...

BUT OUR BOAT WAS GONE! WE COULDN'T FISH ANY MORE!

THE SEA ROSE UP AND SWALLOWED OUR BOAT!

...

THOSE IDIOTS ANGERED THE SEA!

THERE WAS AN OIL SPILL NOT FAR FROM THERE!

IT COULD BE A COINCIDENCE... BUT NOT TOO LONG BEFORE OUR BOAT SANK...

WITH THEIR #@*$ POLLUTION ...!

THEY DID IT ...!

...!

YEAH? YOU'RE GOING ...?

WELL WE BETTER GET GOING!

THANKS FOR THE FISH!

SHAA

FORGET ABOUT ME! SORRY TO BORE YOU!

WELL ANYWAY ...

HEH HEH...I DON'T HAVE TIME FOR SMALL FRY...

HOLD ON A SEC!

YOU'RE NOT GETTING AWAY --!!

TOSS

BUT...

!!

SHU N

YUGI! HALT!

MORE SO IF IT'S A BIG CATCH LIKE YOU!!

I'M NOT DUMB ENOUGH TO LET A FISH GET AWAY AFTER EATING MY BAIT!

HEH HEH! YUGI...

THIS WAY *YOU* GUYS COME TO *ME*-- ON THE BEACH WHERE THE FIGHT'S IN MY FAVOR!

SO I LEFT BAIT FOR HUNGRY DUELISTS LIKE YOU!

HEH! THIS PLACE IS MY *TURF!*

WHAT THE...?!

WHAT DO YOU MEAN, *BAIT* ?

I ACCEPT, KAJIKI!

VERY WELL!

YOU'RE THE CATCH I'M TALKING ABOUT!

YUGI!! LET'S DUEL!

YOU SAYIN' WE'RE FISH?! WHY YOU --!

WHEW... AT LEAST HE'S NOT GONNA *EAT* US...

OH YEAH! IN A FIGHT ON MY TERRAIN, YOU'RE AS GOOD AS ALREADY IN MY NET!

SHAA SHAA SHH

OKAY!

KLIK

I BET TWO STAR CHIPS!

DUEL START!

WSH

BEAT THAT SEA DUDE!

GO YUGI!

READY!!

HERE I GO!!

YUGI	
Life Points	2000

RYOTA KAJIKI	
Life Points	2000

WHAT
...!

WHERE'S
HIS
MONSTER
?!

SPLASH
SPLASH

SPLASH

GO
!!!

NOW...
LIKE I
TOLD YOU,
MY KRAKEN
GETS A
POWER-UP
WHEN IT
FIGHTS
IN THE
SEA!

HOW
CAN I
FIGHT?

HIS CARD'S
THERE...IN
ATTACK
MODE...BUT
THERE'S NO
HOLOGRAM OF
A MONSTER
...!

46

IT WENT BACK UNDER THE WATER!

GG...

SQUID LEGS SUBMISSION HOLD! THE IMP DIES!

GLUP... BLUB... GURG...

BA DAM

YUGI
Life Points **1740**

DOOM

THE SEA STEALTH ATTACK...

HOW CAN I FIGHT MONSTERS I CAN'T EVEN SEE?!

WHEN I'M THROUGH WITH YOU, YOU'LL HAVE A PROPER FEAR AND RESPECT OF THE SEA!

THIS IS PART OF MY FIELD POWER SOURCE! THE SEA STEALTH ATTACK!

DUEL 13: ATTACK FROM THE DEEP

DEVIL KRAKEN
Attack
1560

IMP
Attack
1300

THE KRAKEN SPRANG OUT OF THE WATER BEFORE YUGI'S MONSTER COULD ATTACK! THEN IT DRAGGED YUGI'S MONSTER DOWN WITH IT... AND CRUSHED IT TO DEATH!

IT WENT BACK UNDER THE WATER!

!!

I'M A MASTER OF THE OCEAN DOMAIN! AND WITH THAT COMES THE SEA STEALTH ATTACK!

WA HA HA! SEE THAT, YUGI?

HE CAN'T FIGHT BACK IF HIS ENEMY'S UNDERWATER!

DID YOU SEE THAT?! THAT SQUID THING CAME OUT OF THE WATER WHEN IT ATTACKED!

SHAA AA AA

YUGI!

HIS CARD SKILL IS REALLY GOOD TOO!!

MR. FISH HEAD IN THERE ISN'T JUST SOME WANNA-BE FISHERMAN...

RATS...

BOOM

HMPH...

YUGI

Life Points 1740

DOOM

HEH HEH!

RYOTA KAJIKI

Life Points 2000

YOU STILL HAVEN'T SEEN THE TRUE TERROR OF THE SEA!

THIS IS JUST THE BEGINNING, YUGI!

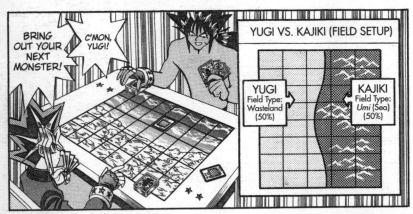

BRING OUT YOUR NEXT MONSTER!

C'MON, YUGI!

YUGI VS. KAJIKI (FIELD SETUP)

YUGI
Field Type: Wasteland (50%)

KAJIKI
Field Type: Umi (Sea) (50%)

FERAL IMP
★★★★★

ATK/1300
DEF/1400

MY BEST MOVE IS TO JUST PUT OUT THIS FERAL IMP IN DEFENSE MODE...

AS LONG AS I CAN'T SEE WHAT I'M FIGHTING...

BUT ON MY NEXT TURN I'LL TEACH YOU A LESSON!

HEH HEH...

ZM ZM

WSH

CRR...

YOU ASKED FOR IT!

I PLAY HORN OF THE UNICORN AND SWITCH THE FERAL IMP TO ATTACK MODE!

COMBO

HORN OF THE UNICORN

A monster equipped with this card increases its ATK and DEF by 700 points.

ZZNT

CRR! CRR!

YUGI'S GOING TO USE ELECTRICITY TO ATTACK THE *WATER ITSELF!*

KAJIKI'S MONSTERS CAN HIDE IN THE SEA ALL THEY WANT, BUT THE FACT THAT THEY'RE *WATER* MONSTERS IS A WEAKNESS AS WELL AS A STRENGTH!

WHAT?

SO *THAT'S* HIS PLAN!

DO IT, GREMLIN!

DA-DOOM

THOSE UNDERWATER MONSTERS ARE IN REAL TROUBLE IF THE WHOLE *OCEAN'S* ELECTRO-CUTED!

WHOA! GOOD IDEA!

SMIRK

ATTACK THE SEA WITH YOUR ELECTRIC SHOCK!

WHAT?!

WHEN THE JELLYFISH IS ON THE BOARD, IT ACTS LIKE A LIGHTNING ROD, NEGATING THE WATER MONSTERS' GREATEST WEAKNESS!

WA HA HA HA!

AND THAT'S NOT ALL!

THE JELLYFISH IS ABSORBING THE ELECTRICITY!

WOBBLE

WOBBLE

IT GETS A POWER BOOST FROM THE SEA!

LEVIATHAN
ATK/2340
DEF/1950

THE WRATH OF LEVIATHAN!

HEH HEH! YES! THE GREAT GOD OF THE PRIMORDIAL OCEAN!

IT'S CUSTOMARY FOR THOSE WHO LIVE OFF THE SEA TO PRAY BEFORE GOING OUT TO FISH...

THOSE WHO ANGER THE GOD FACE HIS WRATH!

DOOSH

SPLASH

SILVER FANG DROWNS!

WH... WHAT THE...?!

Bam

GEEZ! IT'S SO ONE-SIDED...

OH NO! YUGI!

GASP!

YUGI, THAT ATTACK WASN'T INTENDED JUST TO DEFEAT YOUR MONSTER!

HEH HEH!

LOOK DOWN! LOOK AT THE FIELD!

YUGI
Life Points 340

IT'S THE SEA ITSELF! IN ALL ITS ELEMENTAL FURY!

MY ENEMY THIS TIME ISN'T JUST MONSTERS...

GGK...

YOU MAY BE PRETTY TOUGH ON LAND, BUT YOU CAN'T COMPETE WITH THE POWER OF THE SEA!

TOO BAD, YUGI!

MAN! STEALING THE FIELD! I DIDN'T KNOW YOU COULD WIN LIKE THAT...!

COME ON, YUGI!

NORMALLY WHEN I USE LEVIATHAN, IT DOESN'T COVER THIS MUCH OF THE BOARD...BUT I'M SURE NOT GOING TO COMPLAIN!

FUNNY THING, THOUGH...

THERE'S BARELY ANYTHING LEFT OF YUGI'S SIDE OF THE BOARD!

I CAN ONLY PLAY ONE CARD ON THE BOARD...

I ONLY HAVE 5% OF THE FIELD...

...

HERE'S MY CARD!

MY LAST GAMBLE!

WAP

FWP

AWW NO! THEY'VE GOT HIM ON ALL THREE SIDES!

SHAAA

ADVANCE, SEA MONSTERS!

SHAAA

SHAA

NOW IT CAN'T MOVE AT ALL! THERE'S NO WAY FOR YOU TO INCREASE THE SIZE OF THE LAND!

DA-DAM

WAH HA HA HA! MY MONSTERS HAVE SURROUNDED YOUR STONE SOLDIER!

...HÜH?

YESS-SSS! I WIN! I BEAT YUGI ...!

DON'T LAUGH UNLESS YOU'VE GOT SOMETHING TO LAUGH *ABOUT!*

HEH HEH YOUR-SELF!

HEH HEH...

WHAT DO YOU MEAN ?!

YOU'RE TRAPPED! THERE'S NOTHING YOU CAN DO!

KAJIKI! I WAS WAITING FOR THIS MOMENT!

...!

MY MONSTERS ARE SUBMERGED! YOU CAN'T SEE THEM!

YOU SHOULDN'T BE ABLE TO ATTACK THEM AT ALL!

ARE YOU DUMB ?!

I SWITCH THE STONE SOLDIER INTO ATTACK MODE!

PING

HUH ...!?

I DIDN'T SAY I WAS GOING TO ATTACK YOUR MONSTERS ...

HEH HEH ...

SHOOSH

MY MOON CARD CREATED A *HIGH TIDE,* AND IMPROVED YOUR *LEVIATHAN'S* TIDAL WAVE POWER!

THE GRAVITATION OF THE *MYSTICAL MOON* RAISED THE WATER LEVEL! JUST LIKE THE REAL MOON AFFECTS THE OCEAN'S TIDES!

THE *SEA...!* THE TIDE IS PULLING AWAY ...!!

BUT, WHY !?

THE SEA WATER HAS PULLED AWAY, LEAVING YOUR MONSTERS STRANDED HELPLESSLY ON THE SHORE!

TA-DA

NOW THAT THE MOON IS GONE, LEVIATHAN'S POWER IS REDUCED TO HALF OF WHAT IT WAS!

TWCH

TWCH

HE GOT ME...!

HE...HE USED HIS OWN CARD TO HELP ME TAKE OVER HIS TERRAIN?!

WH-WHAT...?!

BURNING LAND

CURSE OF DRAGON
ATK/2000
DEF/1500

COMBO

I'LL USE THIS CARD TO FINISH YOU OFF!!

OUT OF THE WATER, YOUR MONSTERS ARE NOTHING BUT SMALL FRY!

I LOSE!!

WAGGGH!

DIE, MONSTERS, DIE!

KRK

RR

RO

ACCURSED DRAGON! FLAMES OF HELL!

KRKL

RYOTA KAJIKI
Life Points 0

HE CAME FROM BEHIND AND DID IT!

HAHA HAHA! SMELLS LIKE BARBECUED SQUID!

YES!!! YUGI WON!!!

OH WELL... YOU TOOK ME DOWN TO MY LAST STAR CHIP!

BUT I'M NOT OUT OF THE GAME YET! I'VE GOTTA WIN TO AFFORD THAT BIG BOAT!

WAH HA HA HA

I'LL START OVER WITH ONE CHIP! AND EITHER YOU OR ME ARE GONNA WIN!

HEH...

YOU REALLY ARE A BIG FISH!

MAN! YOU REALLY ARE GOOD!

HEH HEH!

YOU'RE NOT BAD YOUR-SELF!

YEAH!

SHAKE

LET'S BOTH DO OUR BEST!!

YUGI
Star Chips: 5

DUEL 14: THE THIEF

GOOD LUCK TO YOU GUYS!

SHAA AA AA

AFTER DEFEATING RYOTA KAJIKI, THE DUELIST OF THE SEA, YUGI AND HIS FRIENDS MOVE ON TO THE NEXT BATTLE...

I GUESS ALL THE DUELISTS ON THIS ISLAND ARE HERE WITH THEIR OWN HOPES AND DREAMS...

THERE'S SOMETHING ABOUT HIM THAT YOU JUST CAN'T HATE!

WHAT A GUY... RYOTA KAJIKI!

US TOO!

...

-- 5 HOURS INTO THE DUELING --

DAM

ALL RIGHT, LET'S GO TO THE NEXT PLACE!

YUGI
Star Chips: 5

JONOUCHI
Star Chips: 2

THAT GUY IN THE SUIT MUST WORK FOR PEGASUS...

OH YEAH...?

THAT'S THE RULES! JUST GIVE UP!

I DON'T CARE HOW YOU LOST THEM! IF YOU RUN OUT OF STAR CHIPS, YOU HAVE TO LEAVE DUELIST KINGDOM!

PLEASE... HELP ME...

OTHER PARTICIPANTS ARE FORBIDDEN TO INTERFERE—UNLESS YOU WANT TO BE DISQUALIFIED TOO!

CAN'T YOU HEAR? HIS CHIPS GOT STOLEN! IT'S NOT THE SAME AS LOSING IN A MATCH!

HEY YOU! LET HIM GO!

I'LL GO AND CATCH HIM FOR YOU!

REALLY?

HEY! WHAT'D THE GUY LOOK LIKE WHO STOLE THEM?

BUT THE MOMENT I PUT DOWN MY CARDS AND STAR CHIPS, HE TOOK THEM AND RAN OFF!

HE CHALLENGED ME TO A DUEL OUT OF NOWHERE...

I COULDN'T SEE HIS FACE, HE HAD A BANDANNA ON IT...

DON'T FORGET! I PROMISE YOU AS A MAN!

I'LL THINK ABOUT IT...

EH...

HE WENT THAT WAY!

WHICH WAY DID HE GO?

HEY YOU! MAN IN BLACK! I'LL GO CATCH THE THIEF -- SO DON'T KICK THIS KID OFF THE ISLAND!

IF I CATCH THAT KID, AS PAYMENT, I'M TAKING HALF YOUR STAR CHIPS!

OH, BY THE WAY!

WHAT?

I WOULDN'T FORGIVE ANYBODY FOR KILLING PEOPLE...OR STEALING STAR CHIPS!

I'LL BEAT HIM UP!!

STAR CHIPS ARE LIKE A DUELIST'S LIFE!

ALL RIGHT, LET'S GO!

MAN, HE'S A TERRIBLE ALTRUIST...

WE WILL CAPTURE HIM AND TAKE HIM BACK TO THE CASTLE!

YMM

YES SIR!

WE'VE TRACKED DOWN THAT KID IN BLOCK "D."

REPEAT! PLEASE SEND ALL PERSONNEL TO BLOCK "D!"

MISTER PEGASUS ...

BEEP

NO STAR CHIPS! OFF THE ISLAND YOU GO!

AND NOW--! YOU'RE COMING WITH ME!

GRIP

W-WAIT!

AGGH ...

WHERE'D THAT THIEF RUN TO NOW...?

TA DA

Pegasus Castle

HOW DROLL AND WITTY CAN YOU BE?!

OH!

HA HA HA HA HA!

OH, MY DEAR FUNNY RABBIT...!

HELP!

HEE OOO

TRULY I AM BLESSED AMONG MEN!

...AND THE WORLD'S BEST COMIC, MADE IN AMERICA... *FUNNY RABBIT!*

THE FINEST WINE... WELL-AGED GORGONZOLA CHEESE...

WHAT IS THE STATUS OF THE DUELS?

BY THE WAY...

THE FIRST SHIP OF EVACUEES WILL BE DEPARTING SHORTLY...

OUT OF 40 PARTICIPANTS, 12 HAVE DROPPED OUT OF THE RACE!

SIR, IT'S SIX HOURS SINCE THE DUELING BEGAN...

YES SIR! HE HAS COLLECTED FIVE STAR CHIPS SO FAR!

OF COURSE, YUGI IS STILL IN THE RUNNING... IS HE NOT?

HE *MUST* MAKE IT TO THE FINALS... SO HE CAN COME TO MY CASTLE!

WOW!

THAT'S MY BOY YUGI!!

OH! WON-DER-FUL!

YOU HAVEN'T FOUND *THAT BOY* YET...HAVE YOU?

AND ONE MORE THING...

I HAVE A GOOD IDEA OF WHAT'S ON HIS MIND...

WELL, THERE'S NO NEED TO WORRY!

TO THINK HE RAN AWAY ...HE MUST REALLY HAVE DISLIKED OUR RECEPTION...

AND AFTER I INVITED HIM TO MY CASTLE AS MY PRIVATE GUEST...

I'M SORRY, SIR. WE TOOK OUR EYES OFF HIM FOR ONLY A MOMENT...

SO FAR, NOT YET...

NO, SIR...

BEFORE TOO LONG, HE'LL SHOW HIMSELF.

KEEP YOUR EYES ON YUGI! THAT'S WHERE OUR GUEST WILL BE HEADED.

FLIP

NOW THEN...

YES SIR!

...LOCK HIM UP IN THE DUNGEON OR SOME-WHERE SO HE DOESN'T GET AWAY!

OH, AND THE NEXT TIME YOU CAPTURE HIM...

HEH HEH...

I WILL BIDE MY TIME UNTIL THE DUEL...

HE'S NOT VERY GOOD AT THIS "WAY OF THE DUELIST" THING...

ARRGGH! IF I FIND THAT KID I CAN GET MY HANDS ON HALF HIS STAR CHIPS!

MAYBE WE SHOULD GIVE UP...

NO MATTER HOW MUCH WE LOOK, WE CAN'T FIND THAT KID!

RATS! WHERE IS HE?

LOOK OVER THERE!

!!

A BOAT OF DUELISTS IS LEAVING THE ISLAND!

HEAVE HO! HEAVE HO!

ROW ROW ROW

HEY! THE KID WHO GOT HIS STAR CHIPS STOLEN IS ON THE BOAT TOO!!

IF MY STAR CHIPS WEREN'T STOLEN...

LISTEN, *ALL OF YOU!* IN CASE YOU DIDN'T KNOW, I'M THE *CHAMPION OF JAPAN!* GIVE ME SOME MORE SPACE!

THOSE WHO LOSE THEIR STAR CHIPS ARE FORCED OFF THE ISLAND!

SO THAT'S THE FATE OF THOSE WHO LOSE THE GAME...

THERE GO MY STAR CHIPS!!

@#$&! THAT GUY IN THE BLACK SUIT BROKE HIS PROMISE!

ROW ROW ROW

YUGI!

MAN, THAT SUCKS...

YUGI!!

LEAP

WHAT THE-!? A BANDAN- NA?!

IT'S *YOU*!

...

DH DOOM

LOOKS LIKE HE'S AFTER *ME*!

HOLD ON, JONOUCHI ...

NOD

KID!

YOU WANT TO DUEL WITH ME?

...

COME WITH ME!

LET'S DO IT IN THAT BATTLE BOX!

OKAY!

DOOM

YUGI...

HE AGREED TO FIGHT HIM JUST LIKE THAT...

HOW MANY STAR CHIPS DO YOU BET?

THAT'S JUST FINE!

ALL MY STAR CHIPS, EH?

THIS KID ISN'T WEARING A DUEL GLOVE...

IT'S SAFE TO SAY HE'S THE THIEF!

I KNEW IT...

KLINK

DADOOM

...

rustle rustle

WHY WOULD HE GO THAT FAR...!?

DID HE STEAL THE STAR CHIPS JUST TO CHALLENGE ME?

THAT MEANS HE WASN'T ONE OF THE DUELISTS CHOSEN TO COME TO THIS ISLAND...

COULD HE BE...?

YUGI KNOWS WHO THAT BOY REALLY IS...

MAYBE...

...SO WHY DID HE ACCEPT THE DUEL?

YUGI'S GOT TO KNOW THAT KID'S THE THIEF...

THIS IS WEIRD!

GET READY, YUGI...

???
Life Points 2000

YUGI
Life Points 2000

DOOM

DUEL!!

MAN-EATING PLANT
ATK/800
DEF/600

WAP

I PLAY THIS CARD!

I KNEW IT! YOU'RE ...

AGGH! LET GO OF ME --!!

MOKUBA !!

FWP

AGH ...!

!! DOOM

DUEL 15: MESSENGER FROM HELL

RRR ....!

DOOM

MOKUBA !!

WHY DID *MOKUBA* TRY TO STEAL YUGI'S STAR CHIPS ....!?

WHAT TH--!? THAT KID'S MOKU-BA!

...ON THIS ISLAND ?!

WHY IS MOKU-BA...

NO!

SLUMP

NOO!

I WON'T GIVE THEM BACK!

I KNOW YOU STOLE TWO OF YUGI'S CHIPS!

MOKUBA, YOU WEASEL!

WHY YOU LITTLE...

GRR RRR

GIVE 'EM BACK! YOU'VE GOT 'EM IN YOUR HAND!

ARE YOU STILL MAD AT YUGI? MO-KUBA...

...!

SO KAIBA'S STILL...

HE'S THE ONE WHO MADE MY BIG BROTHER THE WAY HE IS!

OF... OF COURSE I AM!

THE WORLD'S GREATEST DOCTORS HAVE LOOKED AT HIM BUT...

...THEY SAY HE MIGHT SPEND THE REST OF HIS LIFE LIKE THAT...!

HE'S UNDER 24-HOUR CARE IN THE MANSION...

YES! IN A COMA!

I DIDN'T STEAL THE STAR CHIPS TO GET REVENGE ON YOU!

BUT DON'T GET THE WRONG IDEA...

HMPH...

...

YOU DON'T EVEN KNOW *WHY* PEGASUS HAD THIS TOURNAMENT, DO YOU?

FEH... YOU GUYS THINK YOU'RE SO SMART!

!

PEGASUS WANTS TO BEAT YOU -- AND GAIN CONTROL OF KAIBA CORPORATION!

DOOM

I'LL TELL YOU WHY, YUGI!

!?

WITH THE PRESIDENT OF KAIBACORP IN A COMA, THE STOCK PLUMMETED! THE MANAGEMENT JUST GOT WORSE AND WORSE!

PEGASUS TOOK IT AS AN OPPORTUNITY AND JUMPED IN TO BUY THE COMPANY!

...THE *BIG FIVE*, WHO OWN 60% OF THE COMPANY'S SHARES, HAVE ALL THE DECISION-MAKING POWER!

NOW THAT MY BIG BROTHER IS GONE...

PEGASUS MADE AN OFFER TO THE BIG FIVE... KAIBACORP'S FIVE LEADING STOCK-HOLDERS.

ALL OUR PROBLEMS STARTED BECAUSE OF THAT KID YUGI! THE ONLY WAY TO REGAIN INVESTOR CONFIDENCE IS TO *BEAT YUGI* ONCE AND FOR ALL!

KAIBACORP *DEPENDED* ON THE IMAGE OF KAIBA AS THE *NUMBER ONE GAMER* OF JAPAN!

THE BIG FIVE LIKED HIS OFFER... BUT ON *ONE* CONDITION...

...AND APPOINT *YOU* AS CHIEF EXECUTIVE OF KAIBACORP!

IF *YOU* CAN DEFEAT YUGI, IN AN OFFICIAL GAME OF *DUEL MONSTERS*, WE WILL *DISMISS* THE HALF-DEAD SETO KAIBA...

MISTER PEGASUS!

CONSIDER IT DONE!

BAM
BAM

HEH HEH...

THAT'S IT? I JUST HAVE TO BEAT THIS *BOY*...?

EVEN MY BIG BROTHER TOLD ME HE WAS INVINCIBLE...

NO... NOBODY IN THE WORLD CAN BEAT HIM...

NOT EVEN YOU CAN DEFEAT PEGASUS!

DON'T LAUGH, YUGI!!

SO PEGASUS IS REALLY LOOKING FORWARD TO BEATING ME, ISN'T HE...?

I SEE...

HEH HEH...

...

HE WOULDN'T HAVE LOST A REAL MATCH...SO THE AGREEMENT BETWEEN PEGASUS AND THE BIG FIVE WOULDN'T COUNT!

IF I COULD STEAL ALL OF YUGI'S STAR CHIPS, HE'D BE DISQUALIFIED *BEFORE* HE FOUGHT PEGASUS...

THAT'S WHY I CAME UP WITH MY PLAN...

HEH HEH HEH ...

BECAUSE I HAVE THE KEY!

NO, IT'S NOT!

THE BIG FIVE BROUGHT ME HERE!

SO THAT'S WHY YOU CAME TO THE ISLAND?

HUH? THE KEY TO *WHAT*?

YOU HAVE THE KEY?

SO I *SWALLOWED* THE KEY TO THE SAFE, RIGHT IN FRONT OF THEM!

THEY WERE GOING TO STEAL SOME DOCUMENTS FROM MY BIG BROTHER'S SAFE!

TWO NIGHTS AGO, THE *BIG FIVE* GUYS BARGED INTO MY HOUSE!

THAT'S WHY THEY BROUGHT YOU HERE...? BUT IF THE KEY'S IN YOUR STOMACH...

HAW HEE HEE !

YEAH! EVERY TIME I WENT TO THE BATHROOM, THOSE GUYS WOULD COME RUNNING TO CHECK IT OUT!

IT WAS SOMETHING THEY NEEDED TO COMPLETE THE DEAL WITH PEGASUS!

I WON'T LET THEM HAVE KAIBA CORPORATION EVEN IF THEY TEAR OPEN MY GUTS!

...BUT HIS *REAL* DREAM IS TO BUILD *KAIBA LAND* AMUSEMENT CENTERS ALL OVER THE WORLD SO POOR CHILDREN CAN HAVE FUN!

...MY BIG BROTHER MADE *"DEATH-T"* TO GET REVENGE ON YOU...

YUGI, YOU MIGHT NOT BELIEVE THIS, BUT...

MOKUBA...!

THAT'S WHY HE DEDICATED HIS LIFE TO KAIBA CORPORATION!

SO WHEN HE COMES BACK HE CAN FINISH HIS DREAM!

THAT'S WHY I'LL GIVE MY LIFE TO KEEP IT SAFE!

PLEASE GIVE YUGI HIS STAR CHIPS BACK...!

NOW, CAN YOU BELIEVE IN YUGI?

I BELIEVE IN YOU, MOKUBA.

ALL RIGHT, YUGI!

I'LL TRUST YOU!

NOD!

!!

EXCHANGING STAR CHIPS OUTSIDE A DUEL IS A VIOLATION OF THE RULES! ONE MORE MOVE AND YOU'RE DISQUALIFIED!

STOP RIGHT THERE!

DO

9!

HEH HEH... I FINALLY FOUND YOU, MOKUBA!

YOU SURE LED ME ON A WILD GOOSE CHASE...

THE ONLY WAY TO GET STAR CHIPS IS TO DUEL FOR THEM!

HOW MANY TIMES ARE YOU GOING TO MAKE ME SAY IT?

HOLD IT! TWO OF THOSE STAR CHIPS ARE YUGI'S!

GIVE THEM BACK!

C'MON, GIVE 'EM TO ME!

NOW I'M CONFISCATING YOUR STAR CHIPS!

GRAB

OWW!

THEN I CHALLENGE YOU TO A DUEL!

BUT IF YOU INSIST, I'LL ARRANGE FOR A SPECIAL OPPONENT!

SORRY, I DON'T PLAY GAMES!

HEH HEH...

OVER THERE !

VWIP

!!

WHEN DID THEY GET IN THE DUEL BOX !!

SH—

SH—

SH—

SH—

SH—

SH—

SH—

TH-THAT'S ...!

!!

KAIBA...!?!?

SHOOM

!!

NO!! LOOK CLOSER!

OR.. SOMETHING THAT LOOKS LIKE HIM...

BIG BROTHER...

IT'S JUST A PUPPET THAT LOOKS LIKE KAIBA!

COME IN...COME IN!

AND SOME KIND OF STRANGE VENTRILOQUIST...!

HEE HEE HEE...

Y-Y-YUGI... YOU'LL P-P-PAY FOR WHAT YOU DID TO ME...

R-R-REVENGE... REVENGE... REVENGE!

SH SH

KLATA KLATA

YOU SCUM! MAKING FUN OF KAIBA, ONE OF THE GREATEST DUELISTS I'VE EVER MET!

GRR!

GRR!

GET IN THE BATTLE BOX!!

THAT'S YOUR OPPONENT, YUGI!

I WON'T FORGIVE YOU!

CHOO

KEE KEE KEE...

B-M

THAT'S NOT MY BIG BROTHER! MY BIG BROTHER'S IN THE HOSPITAL!

WHY, YOU LOUSY JERKS!

YUGI!! BEAT THAT GUY UP!

OO OO

TODAY IS THE DAY... I K-K-KILL YOU!

KYA KYA!

RRR !!

THAT PUPPET'S MESSED UP!

COME ON, YUGI! BEAT THAT WEIRDO!

THAT VENTRILOQUIST IS THE FIRST OF THE *ASSASSINS* BROUGHT TO THE ISLAND BY I² TO KILL YOU!

DO YOU REALIZE YET, YUGI? YOUR OPPONENT ISN'T SOME *ORDINARY* DUELIST WHO CAME TO THIS ISLAND FOR THE TOURNAMENT!

HEH HEH HEH ...

AND WHEN THAT HAPPENS, KAIBA CORPORA-TION WILL BELONG TO PEGASUS!

...PUTTING YOU OFF GUARD! LEADING TO YOUR DEFEAT!

THE DOLL WILL DISTURB YOU... ENRAGE YOU...

...

WHAT ...?

BY THE WAY, MOKUBA!

DON'T YOU RECOGNIZE ME?

YOU'RE... YOU'RE *SARUWATARI*, MY BODYGUARD FROM KAIBA CORPORATION!

WHAT?!

BUT EVEN BACK THEN, I WAS ALREADY WORKING FOR INDUSTRIAL ILLUSIONS!

HEH HEH... I'M HONORED YOU REMEMBER ME!

I INFILTRATED KAIBA CORPORATION AS A *SPY!*

HEH HEH... WHILE I WAS *BABYSITTING* YOU, I REPORTED ALL OF KAIBACORP'S CONFIDENTIAL INFORMATION TO MISTER PEGASUS!

HEH HEH HEH HEH!

...JUST YOU WATCH!

AND THAT'S NOT *ALL* I STOLE, MOKUBA...

DUEL 16: THE CARDS BARE THEIR TEETH

DUEL 16: THE CARDS BARE THEIR TEETH

IT CAN'T BE!

THAT'S KAIBA'S BLUE-EYES WHITE DRAGON CARD!!

DH

DOOM

SH

SH SH

KEE KEE KEE!

BLUE-EYES WHITE DRAGON

This legendary dragon is a powerful engine of destruction. Virtually invincible, few have faced this awesome creature and lived to tell the tale.
ATK/3000 DEF/2500

WHAT?!

INDUSTRIAL ILLUSIONS SENT A SPY TO STEAL KAIBA'S CARDS! HE'S GONNA USE THEM TO DEFEAT YOU!

BE CARE-FUL, YUGI!!

EVEN IF YOU DEFEAT *THIS* ASSASSIN, THERE ARE *OTHERS*, MIXED IN WITH THE DUELISTS THAT WERE BROUGHT TO THE ISLAND BY I²!

HEH HEH HEH... THIS IS JUST THE BEGINNING!

YUGI! DON'T LOSE!

THE FIRST PLAYER KILLER IS THE VENTRILO-QUIST OF THE DEAD!!

YOUR OWN GUILT... AND KAIBA'S GRUDGE... WILL SMOTHER YOU! I'LL BURY YOU WITH KAIBA'S OWN CARDS!

KEE KEE KEE!

KEH HEH HEH... YOU CAN'T WIN, YUGI!

THE MOMENT YOU LOSE, PEGASUS GETS KAIBA CORPORA-TION!

YUGI... PLEASE WIN!!

IT'S REALLY M-ME, YUGI... I AM B-B-BORROWING THE B-B-BODY OF THIS DOLL...

TO G-G-GET MY RE-VENGE... BE PRE-PARED...

KEE KEE KEE...

...!

YUGI
Life Points 2000

VENTRILOQUIST OF THE DEAD
Life Points 1200

KAIBA...! WILL YOU ALWAYS BE MY ARCH-RIVAL!?

WHAT IS HE SAYING? IS PART OF KAIBA'S SOUL IN THIS DOLL?! HIS UNDYING GRUDGE...HIS THIRST FOR VENGEANCE?!

GGH...!

DA DOOM

IT'S JUST THE VENTRILO-QUIST, THROWING HIS VOICE!

YUGI! CALM DOWN!

KEE KEE KEE... SOON YOUR M-M-MONSTERS WILL HAVE NOWHERE TO RUN!

BY F-F-FORFEITING MY ATTACK THIS TURN, I CAN P-PLAY THIS CARD FACE DOWN INSTEAD.

L-L-LET'S PLAY MORE! I W-W-WON'T ATTACK YET WITH THE BLUE-EYES WHITE DRAGON...

HMM...! HE PLAYED A CARD FACE DOWN ON THE BOARD...!

IS IT SOME KIND OF SPELL CARD? OR IS IT A TRAP CARD?

I KN-KN-KNEW YOU'D DO THAT!

WHEN YOU PLAY A CARD IN DEFENSE MODE, EVEN IF THE MONSTER IS DESTROYED, THE PLAYER'S LIFE POINTS DON'T DECREASE ...

AND I'LL HAVE TO PLAY THE CURSE OF DRAGON CARD TO THE BOARD IN DEFENSE MODE TOO!

F-FWIP

IT'S MY TURN!

DARK MAGICIAN GOES INTO DEFENSE MODE!

THE DARK MAGICIAN ISN'T POWERFUL ENOUGH TO CHALLENGE THE DRAGON IN AN OFFENSIVE BATTLE ...

FLIP

VWP

TRAP CARD ACTI-VATE!!

TH-THAT'S BECAUSE I'M PLAYING THIS!

BUT IT W-WON'T SAVE YOU...

WHAT?!

**STOP DEFENSE
(Trap Card)**

When your opponent plays a monster in Defense Position, all your opponent's monsters are forced into Attack Position. This is a continuing effect.

STOP DEFENSE!

THIS ISN'T GOOD! AS LONG AS HIS STOP DEFENSE IS ACTIVE, THE BLUE-EYES WHITE DRAGON CAN TEAR RIGHT THROUGH MY MONSTERS TO GET TO ME!

GASP!

NOW ALL YOUR MONSTERS ARE IN ATTACK MODE!

DOM

DOM

SHREE

EEE

GO, BLUE-EYES WHITE DRAGON!

THERE'S NOWHERE TO H-H-HIDE!

KEE KEE KEE ...YES, THAT'S IT!

ANNIHILATE THE ENEMY DRAGON!

BURST STREAM!!

ZGOOO

OOM

BLUE-EYES WHITE DRAGON
Attack
3000 (MAX)

CURSE OF DRAGON
Attack
2000

HOW AM I SUPPOSED TO WIN NOW?!

BAM

NO ....!

YUGI ...

YUGI!

GH ...

OO

OO

YUGI
Life Points
1000

KEE KEE KEE ...

122

MY BIG BROTHER'S NOT DEAD!

KAIBA ISN'T DEAD!

GLEAM

URR...

KAIBA...

I BET KAIBA'S HAPPY-- IF HE'S WATCHING FROM HEAVEN!

HA HA HA HA HA!

I BELIEVED YOU! WHERE IS HE?! I'VE WAITED AND WAITED FOR HIM!

I... BELIEVED ...YOU...

YUGI! YOU TOLD ME THAT MY BIG BROTHER WOULD COME BACK!

YOU'RE RIGHT!

MOKUBA...

I NEVER LOSE!

VSH

I BELIEVE IN KAIBA!!

HMM...?!

HE CLAIMS TO HAVE PLAYED A CARD, BUT *WHERE*?!

THREE TOP HATS...

HEH HEH...

IF YOU CHOOSE THE RIGHT ONE AND DESTROY THE *DARK MAGICIAN*, I LOSE 500 LIFE POINTS!

DID HE HIDE THE CARD IN ANOTHER HAT?!

BUT IF YOU DESTROY THE *WRONG* HAT... YOU'LL ACTIVATE THE *TRAP CARD* I JUST PLAYED!

THE MIDDLE HAT!

I KNOW!

BAM

THE ODDS ARE ONE OUT OF THREE...

A TRAP CARD?!

WHAT...?

HISS

ZGOO

OII

SSS

GOOD CHOICE.

HEH HEH...

BURST STREAM!!

GOOD CHOICE FOR ME, THAT IS!

NO! THE TRAP CARD!

BAM

!!

WHAT'S UNDER THE HAT...?

ZAM

GAM GAM

BLACK MAGIC !!

BLUE-EYES WHITE DRAGON Attack 2300

GAM

'BLUE EYES WHITE DRAGON' DESTROYED !!

DARK MAGICIAN Attack 2500

...

!!

YUGI ...

...!

HE DEFEATED THE WORLD'S RAREST CARD!

HE DID IT !!

BUT HE DID! HE SLEW THE DRAGON !!

HE COULDN'T HAVE ...!

VENTRILOQUIST OF THE DEAD Life Points 700

BURST STREAM!!

INCINERATE THE DARK MAGICIAN!

DA

GOOO!!

I JUST PLAYED THE S-S-SECOND BLUE-EYES WHITE DRAGON!

KEE KEE... WHAT'S THE M-MATTER, YUGI?

BUT HOW?

BUT...

...!

WHAT?!

YUGI
Life Points 500

...

BBMP

I DON'T HAVE A CARD IN MY DECK THAT CAN BEAT THE BLUE-EYES WHITE DRAGON...

I DON'T HAVE A CARD ...

HAVE YOU FORGOTTEN THAT I HAVE TH-THREE BLUE-EYES WHITE DRAGONS?

KEE KEE KEE KEE KEE ...

NOW, P-PLAY YOUR NEXT CARD...SO THE D-DRAGON CAN TURN IT TO A-ASHES!

!!

BAM

...I LOSE...

BA BA BAM

SHREEE SHREEE

GO, DRAGON! DESTROY YUGI!

THEN THIS IS THE END!

WA HA HA HA!

...

GOOD, GOOD, YOU P-P-PLAYED YOUR FINAL CARD, YES?

WHAT'S WRONG ?

...!

HUH ...!?

WHY ISN'T IT ATTACK- ING ...?

DUEL 17:
THE LEGENDARY
DRAGON

THE BLUE-EYES WHITE DRAGON IS *VANISHING*...

...

KAIBA ...!

WH-WHY...

WHY...?

TH-THIS CAN'T BE...

BUT WHY...?

THE BLUE-EYES WHITE DRAGON SELF-DESTRUCTED!

WHAT WAS THAT?! YOU ROCK!

DOOM

HEY! YUGI!

IT WAS ALMOST LIKE KAIBA'S CARD REFUSED TO ATTACK YUGI...

NO MATTER WHY IT HAPPENED, IT MEANS YUGI STILL HAS A CHANCE TO WIN!

UH...I GUESS...

CARDS DON'T THINK! PEOPLE DOES! I MEAN, PEOPLE DO!

GIMME A BREAK, ANZU! SHOWS WHAT YOU KNOW!

A KAIBACORP BATTLE BOX WOULDN'T BREAK THAT EASILY!

YEAH RIGHT, IDIOT!

WHAT IN THE WORLD...? DID THE BATTLE BOX'S VIRTUAL REALITY SYSTEM MALFUNCTION?

YAAY! GO YUGI!

GRR

SERVES THAT CLOWN RIGHT!

HEH!

BIG BROTHER'S CARD CAN'T BE USED JUST BY ANYBODY!

...BUT THERE'S ONE MORE BLUE-EYES WHITE DRAGON IN THAT DECK!

HE MAY HAVE LASTED THIS LONG...

GRR...

KILL THE VENTRILO-QUIST!

YUGI! DO IT!

WHY YOU...

CURSE HIM...

...

VENTRILOQUIST OF THE DEAD

Life Points 700

YUGI

Life Points 500

ENOUGH TALK! LET'S GAME!

I'VE LOST TWO OF THE BLUE-EYES WHITE DRAGON CARDS...THE THIRD IS SOMEWHERE IN THE DECK...

HURRY UP AND PLAY ONE!

THERE'S NO MONSTERS ON YOUR SIDE OF THE BOARD!

IF I CAN DRAW THE LAST BLUE-EYES WHITE DRAGON, MY VICTORY IS ASSURED!

CALM DOWN... A MIRACLE DOESN'T HAPPEN TWICE...

MY TURN!

SO THAT'S IT...YOU'RE TRYING TO PLAY DEFENSE UNTIL YOU DRAW THE BLUE-EYES WHITE DRAGON...

BAM

I PLAY GRAPPLER! DEFENSE MODE!

GRAPPLER
ATK/ 1300
DEF/ 1200

IF HE DRAWS THE BLUE-EYES WHITE DRAGON, I LOSE...

AS LONG AS HIS STOP DEFENSE CARD IS ON THE BOARD, I HAVE TO PLAY MY MONSTERS IN ATTACK MODE...

CELTIC GUARDIAN ★★★★★

ATK/1400
DEF/1200

...AND PLAY THE **CELTIC KNIGHT** IN ATTACK MODE!

I PLACE ONE CARD FACE DOWN ON THE BOARD...

THE ELF SLAYS THE GRAPPLER!

SLASH

SHK

VSH

...

THAT'S FINE. MY LIFE POINTS STAY THE SAME...

HEH HEH...

VENTRILOQUIST OF THE DEAD
Life Points
700

...AND I'LL PLAY A FACE-DOWN CARD TOO!

I PLAY A MONSTER IN DEFENSE MODE...

WHAT IS IT? A SPELL CARD? A TRAP CARD?

HE PLACED ONE OF HIS CARDS FACE DOWN...

FINE! I PLAY *ANOTHER* FACE-DOWN CARD!

VSH

MYSTICAL ELF

ATK/800
DEF/2000

MY TURN IS OVER!

AND I SWITCH THE *MYSTICAL ELF* TO *ATTACK MODE!*

BUT IT DOESN'T MATTER HOW MANY MONSTERS HE HAS! IF I DRAW THE BLUE-EYES WHITE DRAGON AND KILL JUST ONE OF THEM, HIS LIFE POINTS WILL HIT ZERO!

TWO CARDS FACE DOWN, AND THREE MONSTERS ON THE BOARD...

IT'S SO THICK WITH TENSION, IT'S SUFFOCATING JUST TO WATCH IT!

WHEW! THERE'S A BAD VIBE IN THERE...

THE CARD THAT'LL DECIDE THE DUEL...

FACE-DOWN CARDS ON BOTH SIDES...!

I BET ONE OF THEM IS THE TRUMP CARD...

PLEASE WIN!

YUGI!

YUGI WILL WIN!

DON'T WORRY!

PLEASE!! BEAT BIG BROTHER'S CARD JUST THIS ONCE ...!

YUGI!

YUGI ....!

!!

SLAUGHTER THE HOLY ELF!

BURST STREAM OF DESTRUCTION!

IT'S OVER!

NEGATE ATTACK
(Trap Card)

When your opponent attacks, negate the attack and make your opponent's Battle Phase end.

FLIP

I PLAY A SPELL CARD!

SMIRK

SHOOOO

SHOOOO

SHOOOO

THE REFLECTED BURST STREAM IS SUCKED AWAY INTO HOLES IN SPACE-TIME!

NEGATE ATTACK!

I'M ALWAYS ONE STEP AHEAD OF YOU!

KEH HEH... YOUR TRUMP CARD ENDED UP BEING USELESS ...

HE ANTICI-PATED MY TRAP CARD...

@#$&...

IT'S OVER...

YUGI!

WHAT NOW?!

HERE'S MY *NEXT* TRUMP CARD.

HEH HEH...

YOU MUST BE AT YOUR WITS' END...

NOW YUGI, IT'S YOUR LAST TURN!

WHAT!?

!

MONSTER REBORN

MONS-TER RE-BORN!!!

IMPOSSIBLE! IS HE GOING TO BRING ONE OF MY CARDS BACK FROM THE DEAD...?!

WRONG, THIEF!

I'M NOT BRINGING BACK YOUR CARD...

...IT'S KAIBA'S CARD!!

DA

DUN

ZU ZU

I HAVE NO CHOICE... THE EQUALLY MATCHED BLUE-EYES WHITE DRAGONS WILL HAVE TO KILL ONE ANOTHER!

CURSE HIM! CURSE HIM!

THE DRAGON!

154

HEH HEH... MR. VENTRILO-QUIST...

MAY YOUR PUPPET BE A MERCIFUL MASTER IN THE ILLUSION I'VE TRAPPED YOU IN...!

TWITCH TWITCH

AGGH! GYAA! HELP ME! HELP ME!

DOO!

GYA-AAA-AGH!

M!

MOKUBA...!

I GOT KAIBA'S CARDS BACK, TOO!

NOW YOU'VE MADE UP FOR THE STAR CHIPS YOU LOST!

YOU DID IT, YUGI!!

RATS! DID THEY TAKE HIM TO THE CASTLE?

HE'S GONE!

WHAT?!

...HOLD ON. WHERE'D MOKUBA GO?

YUGI
Star Chips 6

KAIBA MANOR

SLAM

PREPARE THE CHOPPER!

WHP

MASTER SETO! PLEASE WAIT!

WHERE ARE YOU GOING? YOU CAN'T JUST RUN OFF!

YOU'RE STILL NOT WELL ENOUGH TO...

BE QUIET!

WHP WHP

MOKUBA WAS ABDUCTED WHILE YOU FOOLS WERE SUPPOSED TO BE GUARDING HIM!

SIR!

WE'RE SORRY, MASTER SETO!

DUEL 18: ON MY OWN

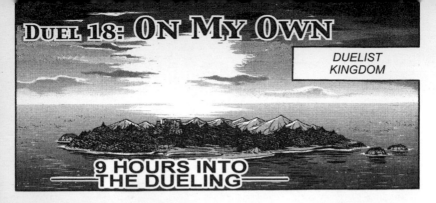

DUELIST KINGDOM

9 HOURS INTO THE DUELING

MOKUBA...

WHAT CAN WE DO TO HELP HIM *NOW*?

DO YOU THINK THEY TOOK HIM TO PEGASUS'S CASTLE?

I CAN'T FIND MOKUBA ANY-WHERE!

HE'S GONE!

MAN, I'VE GOT TO GET MORE STAR CHIPS...

BOOM

JONOUCHI
Star Chips 2

WHOOM

YUGI
Star Chips 6

YOU SAID IT!

WE'LL JUST HAVE TO COLLECT 10 STAR CHIPS AND GET TO PEGASUS'S CASTLE!

SETO KAIBA

President of Kaiba Corporation

Defeated by Yugi in his own "Death-T" (Theme Park of Death), he is sent into a coma by Yugi's "Mind Crush" power. Now, he has regained consciousness and is headed to Pegasus' island for reasons known only to himself.

YUGI & JONOUCHI

Yugi wants to defeat Pegasus to release his grandfather's soul, which Pegasus trapped inside a videotape.

Jonouchi wants to defeat Pegasus so he can win the prize money and pay for his little sister's eye surgery.

DUELISTS REMAINING: 29

DUEL FIELD

MAI KUJAKU •
PRIZE HUNTER

DUEL 18: ON MY OWN

PEGASUS J. CRAWFORD

Nationality: American • Age: 24

Genius game designer and President of I² (Industrial Illusions), the colossal game company which sells the collectible card game "Duel Monsters." Under the pretext of a "Duel Monsters" tournament, he invited Yugi to his island to defeat him. Like Yugi, he possesses a Millennium Item, the mysterious Millennium Eye.

PEGASUS CASTLE

MOKUBA KAIBA

In his stomach is the key to a safe containing important documents regarding the sale of KaibaCorp. He is currently confined in Pegasus' castle.

KAIBA CORPORATION "BIG FIVE"

The secret executive group of KaibaCorp. They plan to fire Seto Kaiba and sell the corporation to Pegasus…on the condition that Pegasus beats Yugi.

ZAPAM

YAWN... ATTACK, HARPY QUEENS...

TRIANGLE ECSTASY SPARK!

AGGGH! NOOO!

DOO

NOW GIVE ME YOUR STAR CHIPS AND BEAT IT...!

THERE. YOU HAPPY? I WIN...

I JUST CAN'T GET INTO IT...

SIGH

BO-RING...

HO HUM

SOB! NOW I'M OUT OF THE TOURNAMENT!

IT'S WHAT YOU CAN SHOW... BUT YOU CAN'T SEE!

THERE'S ONE THING THAT DOESN'T CHANGE...

IT'S SO IRRITAT-ING!

AND THAT STUPID SAYING! I HAVE NO IDEA WHAT IT MEANS!

THE WHOLE WORLD SHOULD BLOW UP BEFORE THAT HAPPENS!

I CAN'T BELIEVE I LOST TO SOMEBODY LIKE HIM!

ARRGH! THAT PISSES ME OFF!

GRRR

HUH...?

I FINALLY FOUND YOU! MAI KUJAKU!!

UM...A BALD GUY WEARING A TOUPEE?

WHAT'S SOMETHING YOU CAN SHOW BUT YOU CAN'T SEE?

A SKINNY GIRL WITH A "D" CUP?

NO, THAT'S NOT IT...

MUTTER MUTTER

SHF

THANKS FOR MAKING A FOOL OUT OF ME ON THE SHIP!

DINOSAUR RYUZAKI, THE WORLD'S GREATEST DUELIST!

IT'S ME!

ANOTHER IRRITATION...

@#$%...

WHAT'D YOU SAY?! WHY YOU...

GRR...

MAKING FUN OF ME AGAIN, EH...?

I'M NOT INTERESTED IN FIGHTING SOMEBODY I'VE ALREADY BEATEN ONCE!

SHUT UP!

GET LOST!

SHOO

PLAY ME ONE MORE TIME RIGHT HERE!

WHAT THE ....!?
SHE'S GOT EIGHT STAR CHIPS ALREADY!

WSH

I EVEN HAVE *FIVE* STAR CHIPS ALREADY!

LISTEN! IN CASE YOU FORGOT, I WAS THE RUNNER-UP IN THE LAST TOURNAMENT, OUT OF EVERYONE IN JAPAN!

I'M GOING TO *WIN* THIS TIME!

BUT DON'T BE AFRAID...

TWO MORE STAR CHIPS AND I'LL BE IN PEGASUS'S CASTLE!

YOU GET IT?

BUT *BEFORE* I DO THAT... THERE'S ANOTHER GUY I HAVE TO TAKE DOWN...

WHO IS IT? YUGI?

HMPH...

I'M THE ONE WHO'S GOING TO BEAT *HIM*!

...I'VE ALREADY DECIDED WHO I'M GOING TO GET MY LAST TWO STAR CHIPS FROM!

AND BELIEVE ME, HE'S NOT A LOSER LIKE YOU!

...!

WAIT A SEC

YOU HAVE TO BEAT SOMEONE FOR ME FIRST!

BUT UNDER ONE CONDITION!

ALL RIGHT, RYUZAKI!

I'LL DUEL WITH YOU.

YOU MEAN IT?

I HATE DOING ANYTHING FOR HER, BUT IF I'VE GOT TO, I'VE GOT TO...

GRR...

WH-WHAT?!

UNTIL YOU BEAT HIM, YOU'RE MY SLAVE! YOU GOT THAT?

OH, ONE MORE THING!

SO WHO IS THIS GUY YOU HATE SO MUCH?

I'LL DO IT!

COME WITH ME!

TAKOYAKI = A JAPANESE SNACK FOOD MADE OF FRIED OCTOPUS COVERED IN BATTER.

THAT ONE'S EASY!

OH! I KNOW! IT'S THE OCTOPUS IN A PIECE OF TAKOYAKI!*

...!?

WHAT IS THIS, A QUIZ?

RIDDLE ME THIS: WHAT'S "SOMETHING THAT YOU CAN SHOW, BUT YOU CAN'T SEE?"

BY THE WAY...

I'M SICK OF YOUR BOSSY TONE OF VOICE!

GRR...

COME ON, SLAVE!

IT WAS STUPID OF ME TO ASK.

WANNA DUEL WITH ME?

HEY YOU!

AGGH! HE GOT AWAY AGAIN!

W-WAIT!

THAT'S THE FOURTH PERSON!

I'LL PASS... I DON'T WANT TO HAVE TO FIGHT YUGI NEXT...

THAT GUY WITH YOU... HE'S YUGI, ISN'T HE?

LOOOM

!

THOSE COWARDS...!

SHAKE

SHAKE

I DON'T BELIEVE IT... THE OTHER PLAYERS JUST SEE YUGI'S FACE AND RUN AWAY...

OHO HO HO HO!

I RECOGNIZE THAT LAUGH!

SHUT UP! I DON'T SEE YOU DUELING!

URK

BUT IF WE LET HIM GO OFF BY HIMSELF HE'LL PROBABLY GET HIS BUTT KICKED...

THIS IS A PROBLEM. WE CAN'T GET ANYONE TO FIGHT JONOUCHI...

IT KINDA FEELS GOOD...

EVERYBODY'S AFRAID OF YUGI...

IT'S MAI KUJAKU!!!

ULP...

HEH HEH HEH!

IT'S YOU! THE HARPY LADY!

DOOM

WE MEET AGAIN, JONOUCHI!

PBB

W-WE'RE NOT DUCKLINGS!

DO YOU ALL WALK IN A LINE, TOO? MAYBE YOU WERE DUCKLINGS IN YOUR PAST LIFE?

I SEE THAT YOU GUYS ARE GLUED AT THE HIP, AS USUAL!

THIS WOMAN...

...

I BET IF YOU WERE ALONE, YOU'D HAVE BEEN AT THE CASTLE A LONG TIME AGO!

BE HONEST, YUGI...ISN'T IT A NUISANCE TO HAVE ALL THESE PEOPLE TAILING AFTER YOU?

168

MY REAL TARGET IS...

NOW IS NOT THE TIME TO FIGHT HIM...

OOPS... HE LOOKS MAD. I'D BETTER BACK OFF ON PROVOKING YUGI...

YOUR SLAVE?!

BAM

TA DAA!

JONO-UCHI!

I LET YOU DEFEAT ME LAST TIME...

...BUT THIS TIME YOU HAVE TO FIGHT MY SLAVE!

BAGOOOOM

A POWERHOUSE PLAYER WHO WAS THE RUNNER-UP OF THE PREVIOUS TOURNAMENT! CAN JONOUCHI BEAT HIM?

DINO-SAUR RYU-ZAKI!!

HOW YOU DOING, JONO-UCHI?

HEH HEH... LONG TIME NO SEE, YUGI!

WHAT A SUCKER... DEPENDING ON HOW YOU LOOK AT IT, MAYBE I SHOULD THANK MAI KUJAKU...

HEH HEH...

ROAA

I'LL TAKE YOU ON!!

I'M NOT A DUCKLING!

JONOUCHI, WAIT! LET'S THINK ABOUT THIS!

I WISH I COULD PLAY YOU AGAIN AND WIN BACK MY STARS BY MYSELF...BUT THAT WOULD BE A LITTLE IMMATURE. IF RYUZAKI BEATS JONOUCHI, AND I BEAT RYUZAKI, THEN IT'S THE SAME AS BEATING THEM BOTH!

WHAT A SIMPLE GUY...

HEH HEH...

GRR

IT'S OBVIOUS SHE'S AFRAID OF LOSING TO YUGI!

WHY IS SHE GOING AFTER JONOUCHI?

WHAT'S THE MATTER WITH HER?!

I'LL DO IT!

RMM BB

HEH HEH...

WAIT AND SEE! YUGI WILL SUPPORT JONOUCHI LIKE HE DID LAST TIME!

MAI KUJAKU! I WILL LEAD JONOUCHI TO VICTORY!!

GET HIM, RYUZA-KIII--IIII!

I'LL BE THERE WAITING FOR YOU!

YEAH!

IS THAT BATTLE BOX OKAY WITH YOU?

!

I HAVE A FAVOR TO ASK YOU.

YUGI!

THIS DUEL...I DON'T WANT YOU TO GIVE ME ANY ADVICE.

HE'S NOT SOMEBODY YOU CAN BEAT AT YOUR SKILL LEVEL!

ARE YOU NUTS?!

JONO-UCHI!! WHAT ARE YOU SAYING?!

I WON'T BE ABLE TO SAVE SHIZUKA...

IF I BET ALL MY STAR CHIPS IN THIS DUEL AND I LOSE, IT'S ALL OVER...

BUT...

IN MY MIND I'M YELLING AT MYSELF "WHAT ARE YOU DOING, YOU IDIOT?"

"WHY DID YOU SAY THAT? TAKE IT BACK!"

IT'S PRETTY DUMB OF ME, HUH?

...I WANT TO WIN ON MY OWN!

JONO-UCHI ...!

WIN THIS DUEL BY YOUR OWN HANDS!

I KNOW WHAT YOU MEAN, JONO-UCHI.

...SHIZUKA CAN WIN TOO!!

IF I CAN WIN...

THAT'S HOW I FEEL!!

YUGI'S BACK TO NORMAL...!

YUGI!

BLINK

Y-YEAH...

YOU'RE RIGHT!

C'MON GUYS! LET'S ALL ROOT FOR JONOUCHI!

CHOOM

THANK YOU... BOTH OF YOU...

YUGI...

AH?

GOOD LUCK JONO-UCHI!!

I'M GOING!

AND AS PROOF OF HIS TRUST, HE HID HIMSELF IN YUGI'S HEART...

THE OTHER YUGI ACCEPTED JONOUCHI'S WISHES...

I THINK I KNOW WHY YUGI'S BACK TO NORMAL...

HE'S HELPING JONOUCHI LEARN TO BE MORE CONFIDENT...

BY TRUSTING HIS FRIEND AND STAYING OUT OF THE FIGHT...

YUP!

DASH

LET'S CHEER FOR JONO-UCHI!

C'MON YUGI!

NOW THAT THE OTHER YUGI'S GONE, I'M ACTUALLY WORRIED...

OH NO...

B-BMP

B-BMP

THE AUDIENCE IS PRETTY LIVELY, HUH?

HEH...

BY THE WAY, HOW MANY STAR CHIPS ARE WE GOING TO WAGER?

MAKE HIS DUMB DINOSAURS EXTINCT!

YOU CAN DO IT, JONO-UCHI--!

THERE'LL BE A PRIZE FOR YOU IF YOU WIN!

BEAT HIM, MY FAITHFUL SLAVE!

MY DINOSAUR CARDS WILL GET A POWER-UP BECAUSE OF THE *WASTELAND* SQUARES.

THIS FIELD IS PART *WASTE-LAND* AND PART *GRASS-LAND!*

GET READY, OKAY?

ALL RIGHT! TWO FOR ME TOO.

ALL TWO OF THE STAR CHIPS I HAVE!!

ALL OF THEM!

WAP

YOUR DINOSAUR DECK'S PROBABLY PRETTY STRONG...YOU TOOK SECOND PLACE IN THE TOURNAMENT... BUT...

RYUZAKI...

DUEL!!

LET'S START!

DINOSAUR RYUZAKI
Life Points 2000

JONOUCHI
Life Points 2000

THE DEADLY MOVE OF TURNING THE BABY DRAGON INTO THE SUPER-STRONG THOUSAND DRAGON USING THE TIME WIZARD!

...I HAVE THE *ULTIMATE COMBO* THAT BEAT MAI KUJAKU!

TIME WIZARD

BABY DRAGON ★★★★
ATK/120
DEF/7

GO FOR IT, JONOUCHI!

SMASH JONO-UCHI!

GET HIM, SLAVE!

HEH HEH... I'VE ALREADY WON!

I CAN'T BELIEVE IT! I DREW BABY DRAGON AND TIME WIZARD ALREADY!

LUCKY!!

YEAH!

HEH HEH! PLAY WHATEVER MONSTER YOU WANT! ON MY NEXT TURN I'LL PLAY THE *TIME WIZARD* AND YOUR DINOSAURS WILL BE DEAD MEAT!

I PLAY THE BABY DRAGON! IN DEFENSE MODE!

I GO FIRST!

VSH

BABY DRAGON

ATK/1200
DEF/700

I PLAY THIS!

TWO-HEADED KING REX!

HUH...?

GRAAR

TWO-HEADED KING REX

ATK/1600
DEF/1200

JONO-UCHI!

MAN...THIS DINOSAUR THING LOOKS REALLY TOUGH!

GRAA AAA

DON'T LOSE, JONO-UCHI!

BA BAM

GGK...

THE MATCH IS ALREADY DECIDED!

TALK ABOUT A NEWBIE!

OHO HO HO HO HO!

Duel 19: I Won't Lose!

THAT WAS MY TRUMP CARD!

WHA...!

STOMP STOMP

DA DUN

HEH HEH... IDIOT!

SPLAT

RYUZAKI'S **TWO-HEADED KING REX** INSTANTLY SMASHES JONOUCHI'S **BABY DRAGON!**

SO, JONOUCHI! YOU WERE GOING TO DO THE SAME THING TO HIM THAT YOU DID TO ME? WELL, JUST **TRY** AGING YOUR BABY DRAGON AFTER YOU **SCRAPE IT** OFF OF KING REX'S FOOT!

OHO HO HO HO HO!

THIS ISN'T GOOD...!

MY PLAN IS RUINED!

GULP...

GET HIM, RYUZAKI BABY! HE'S JUST A BEGINNER!

DON'T GIVE UP!

JO-NO-UCHI!

GRR...

C'MON! HURRY UP AND PLAY YOUR NEXT CARD!

YOU CAN'T LOSE TO HIM! HIS THEME DECK SUCKS!

YOU CAN STILL WIN, JONO-UCHI!

MAN, THIS MONSTER IS BIG...!

TWO-HEADED KING REX

★★★★★★

ATK/1600
DEF/1200

MY DINOSAUR DECK CAN BEAT ANY-THING!

HEH HEH...

DINOSAUR RYUZAKI

Life Points 2000

ALL RIGHT, ALL RIGHT...

JONOUCHI

Life Points 2000

YOUR GUY'S PRETTY TOUGH BUT...

...I HAVE A STRONG CARD IN MY HAND TOO!!

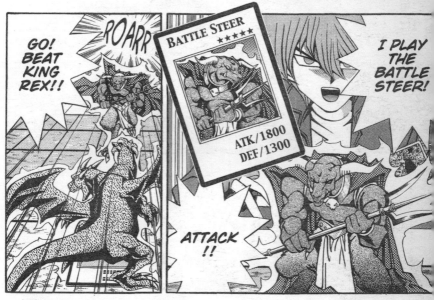

GO! BEAT KING REX!!

ROARR

BATTLE STEER ★★★★

ATK/1800
DEF/1300

I PLAY THE BATTLE STEER!

ATTACK!!

AHA HA HA! FLATTEN HIM!

OH NO... I FORGOT ABOUT THE FIELD POWER SOURCE!

D DOOM

A MEASLY 1800 ATTACK POINTS? DON'T YOU KNOW MY TYRANNOSAURUS GETS A POWER-UP BECAUSE OF THE WASTELAND?

HA HA HA! YOU DIMWIT

CRIPES ...

JONOUCHI
Life Points **1720**

TWO-HEADED KING REX
Attack **2080**

DINO-SAUR FOOT STOMP!!

S MASH

TAKE YOUR TIME, JONOUCHI! DON'T RUSH!

I CAN'T FORGET MY REAL GOAL... TO BEAT MAI KUJAKU! I'LL FINISH THIS IDIOT OFF... QUICK.

YEAH, YEAH.

IF YOU BEAT JONOUCHI, WE CAN HAVE A SPECIAL DUEL, JUST YOU AND ME!

OHH RYU-ZAAA-KI!!

AXE RAIDER
ATK/1700
DEF/1150

FIELD POWER SOURCE: GRASS-LAND!

HERE'S MY NEXT CARD!

THAT'S GOOD TERRAIN FOR WARRIORS AND KNIGHTS! AND I HAVE A LOT OF THEM!

MY SIDE OF THE BOARD IS SOGEN... GRASS-LAND!

JONO-
UCHI!

GIVE IT UP, DUDE! YOU'LL HAVE TO TAKE EARTH BACK TO THE *ICE AGES* BEFORE YOU BEAT MY DINOSAUR CARDS!

HA HA HA!

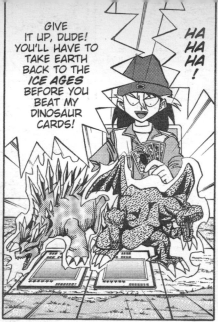

HE PLAYED A DINOSAUR CARD WITH AN *EVEN STRONGER* ATTACK POWER!

!!

JONOUCHI
Life Points **1145**

JONOUCHI WILL LOSE IF THIS KEEPS UP...!

AM I JUST NOT GOOD ENOUGH TO BEAT HIM...?

AWW MAN...

YUGI...

GLANCE

I NEED...

SLAP

SHEESH!

I CAN'T ASK YUGI FOR HELP ALL THE TIME!

HOW PATHE-TIC!

AHooo ☆

IT'S A PROMISE TO MYSELF!

STING

I'M GONNA WIN ON MY OWN!!

WHAT DO I DO...?

NONE OF THE CARDS IN MY HAND ARE GOOD ENOUGH TO BEAT HIS DINO-SAURS!

TIME WIZARD

★★★★

★★★

RE GROTTO #1

★★★★

MY TURN!

DOES IT HAVE SOME OTHER POWER HIDDEN IN IT ...?

BUT I DON'T KNOW ANY OTHER WAY TO USE IT EXCEPT THE COMBO I USED TO BEAT MAI KUJAKU...

THE TIME WIZARD HAS THE POWER TO CONTROL TIME...TAKE IT FORWARD OR BACKWARDS ...

YUGI GAVE ME THIS CARD...

TIME WIZARD

I'LL PLAY IT FACE DOWN ON THE TABLE FOR NOW...

ALL RIGHT... IT MIGHT COME IN HANDY SOMEHOW ...

BUT KNOWING THIS BOY, HE PROBABLY PLAYED IT WITHOUT EVEN KNOWING HOW TO USE IT...

IT'S SAFE TO SAY THAT THAT CARD IS THE *TIME WIZARD!*

IT'S COOL! HE DOESN'T EVEN KNOW HOW TO USE IT!

YEAH, I KNOW!

JONOUCHI JUST PLAYED THE *TIME WIZARD!*

RYU-ZAKI!

THE TIME WIZARD ...!

JONO-
UCHI!

JONO-
UCHI!

WA HA
HA HA!
DO YOU
GIVE UP
YET?

!!

I DON'T
KNOW
WHAT
HE CAN
DO
TO BEAT
THEM
...!

WITH THE
FIELD POWER
ON THEIR
SIDE, THOSE
DINOSAUR
CARDS ARE
JUST TOO
TOUGH FOR
JONOUCHI TO
FIGHT!

JONOUCHI

Life
Points 665

GH...

THERE
MAY
BE *ONE*
WAY...

THERE'S
ONE
CARD
...

ISN'T
THERE
A WAY FOR
JONOUCHI
TO BEAT
RYUZAKI
?

YUGI
!

THERE'S A CHANCE... IF JONOUCHI USES THE TIME WIZARD

BUT IT'S RISKY... AND WILL HE REALIZE IT...?

TIME WIZARD

YEAH, YUGI!

OTHERWISE HE'S GOING TO LOSE!

...

TELL JONOUCHI WHAT TO DO!

PLEASE, YUGI!

DON'T YOU SEE, YUGI?

...

IF HE LOSES, IT'S ALL OVER FOR HIM!

JONOUCHI TOLD YOU NOT TO GIVE HIM ANY ADVICE, AND YOU DON'T WANT TO BREAK YOUR PROMISE. BUT...

I KNOW WHY YOU DON'T WANT TO SAY ANYTHING.

KIND-NESS...!!

I KNOW YOU WANT TO PROTECT JONOUCHI'S HONOR, BUT WOULDN'T TRUE KINDNESS BE TO LEND HIM A HAND RIGHT NOW...?

THINK ABOUT JONOUCHI'S SISTER! WHAT WILL HAPPEN TO HER IF HE LOSES...?

YUGI!

JONO-UCHI!!

FOOM

WHAT...?

JO...

ALL RIGHT! I'LL TELL YOU!

196

DON'T SAY **ANYTHING** TO JONOUCHI! WE CAN'T INTERFERE IN THIS BATTLE.

!!

MY OTHER SELF ...!?

IF WE RESCUE HIM FROM THIS SITUATION, **THAT'S** WHEN JONOUCHI WILL **TRULY LOSE!**

NO!

BUT IF THIS GOES ON, JONOUCHI WILL...!

FOR **JONO-UCHI**, THIS IS A BATTLE AGAINST **HIM-SELF**.

HUH ...!?

WE MUST WATCH THE COURAGE OF JONOUCHI, WHO DROVE HIMSELF INTO A CORNER AND TOOK THIS CHALLENGE OF HIS OWN FREE WILL!

THE ONLY THING WE CAN DO IS WATCH.

SHIZUKA CAN WIN TOO!

IF I CAN WIN...

THAT'S HOW I FEEL!

YOU'RE RIGHT!

YEAH...

STARE !

THOSE AREN'T THE EYES OF SOMEBODY WHO'S GIVEN UP THE FIGHT!!

AND BESIDES.. LOOK AT HIS EYES!

GO FOR IT, MAN!

JONO-UCHI... YOU'RE SO...

JO-NO-UCHI!!

FLAME SWORDSMAN ★★★★★

FIELD POWER SOURCE: GRASS-LAND!

ATK/1800 DEF/1600

WHAM

I PLAY THIS CARD!

VSH

MY TURN!

TO BE CONTINUED IN
YU-GI-OH!: DUELIST VOL. 3!

BONUS!

Battle Trump Game

○ THIS IS A STRATEGIC BATTLE GAME FOR TWO PLAYERS USING REGULAR PLAYING CARDS! (BASICALLY, IT'S CARD CHESS.) THE PLAYERS TAKE TURNS MOVING THEIR CARDS AND FIGHTING. TO WIN, YOU MUST TRAP YOUR OPPONENT'S JOKER. LEARN THE RULES AND PLAY IT WITH YOUR FRIENDS!

WHAT YOU NEED:

○ A DECK OF ORDINARY PLAYING CARDS
○ A BIG PIECE OF PAPER WITH A 5X5 GRID DRAWN ON IT (SEE THE NEXT PAGE) (OPTIONAL)
○ NINE COINS

PREPARATIONS BEFORE PLAYING

○ FOR THIS GAME, YOU ONLY NEED THE 2S, 3S, 4S, 5S, ACES AND TWO JOKERS. REMOVE ALL THE OTHER CARDS FROM THE DECK. IF YOUR DECK OF CARDS DOESN'T HAVE JOKERS, USE TWO KINGS INSTEAD.

○ PREPARE A 5X5 GRID (SEE BELOW). THE SQUARES OF THE GRID SHOULD BE BIG ENOUGH TO FIT CARDS IN THEM. YOU DON'T HAVE TO DRAW THE GRID AS LONG AS IT'S CLEAR WHERE THE SQUARES ARE.

} PLAYER 1'S SIDE

} PLAYER 2'S SIDE

HOW TO PLAY

○ EACH PLAYER PLACES ONE JOKER CARD, FACE UP, ANYWHERE ON THEIR SIDE. (THE JOKER IS LIKE THE KING IN CHESS.)

○ SHUFFLE THE OTHER 20 CARDS (ACES, 2S, 3S, 4S AND 5S) AND PLACE THEM IN A SINGLE STACK.

○ EACH PLAYER DRAWS 8 CARDS FROM THE STACK, TAKING TURNS. HOWEVER, EVEN AFTER YOU DRAW THEM, *YOU CAN'T LOOK AT YOUR OWN CARDS!*

○ PLAYERS PLACE THE 8 CARDS FACE DOWN ON THEIR OWN SIDES, TAKING TURNS. YOU CAN'T PUT MORE THAN ONE CARD ON THE SAME SPACE.

○ PLACE A COIN ON EACH OF PLAYER 1'S CARDS (SO YOU CAN TELL THEM APART FROM PLAYER 2'S CARDS).

○ USE ROCK-PAPER-SCISSORS TO DECIDE WHO GOES FIRST.

○ WHEN THE GAME STARTS, THE PLAYERS TAKE TURNS. ON YOUR TURN, YOU MUST DO *ONE* OF THE FOLLOWING (NOT BOTH!):

- FLIP OVER ONE OF YOUR OWN FACE-DOWN CARDS SO IT'S FACE-UP.
- MOVE ONE OF THE FACE-UP CARDS. EACH CARD MOVES DIFFERENTLY BASED ON ITS NUMBER (ACE, 2, 3, 4, ETC.), AND FIGHTS DIFFERENTLY BASED ON ITS SUIT (HEARTS, DIAMONDS, ETC.). IF YOU MOVE INTO A SPACE WITH THE OTHER PLAYER'S CARD, YOU MUST STOP AND FIGHT THEM.

MOVEMENT AND BATTLE

CARD MOVEMENT

JOKER / A	CAN MOVE *ONE SPACE* IN ANY DIRECTION
2	CAN MOVE *UP TO TWO SPACES* LEFT, RIGHT, UP OR DOWN
3	CAN MOVE *UP TO THREE SPACES* DIAGONALLY
4	CAN MOVE *UP TO FOUR SPACES* LEFT, RIGHT, UP OR DOWN
5	CAN MOVE *UP TO FIVE SPACES* DIAGONALLY

CARD BATTLE

WIN ♡ WIN
♣ TIE TIE ♠
TIE TIE
WIN ◇ WIN

♡ ...... ELEMENT OF FIRE
♠ ...... ELEMENT OF WOOD
◇ ...... ELEMENT OF EARTH
♣ ...... ELEMENT OF WATER

WHEN TWO CARDS FIGHT, THE WINNER IS DETERMINED BY THE SUIT (HEARTS, DIAMONDS, ETC.). USE THIS CHART TO SEE WHO WINS.

♡ ... BEATS ♠ LOSES TO ♣

♠ ... BEATS ◇ LOSES TO ♡

◇ ... BEATS ♣ LOSES TO ♠

♣ ... BEATS ♡ LOSES TO ◇

JOKER ... ♡ · ♠ · ◇ · ♣
LOSE TO ANY CARD. JOKERS CAN ONLY ATTACK THE ENEMY JOKER.

	♡	♠	◇	♣
♡	BOTH CARDS DIE	HEART BEATS SPADE	TIE	CLUB BEATS HEART
♠	HEART BEATS SPADE	BOTH CARDS DIE	SPADE BEATS DIAMOND	TIE
◇	TIE	SPADE BEATS DIAMOND	BOTH DIE	DIAMOND BEATS CLUB
♣	CLUB BEATS HEART	TIE	DIAMOND BEATS CLUB	BOTH DIE

BATTLE SYSTEM

- ○ MOVE YOUR CARDS ACCORDING TO THEIR NUMBER (SEE PAGE 206). YOU CAN JUMP OVER YOUR OWN CARDS WHILE MOVING, BUT YOU CAN'T STOP ON THE SAME SPACE WITH THEM. YOU CAN'T JUMP OVER YOUR OPPONENT'S CARDS! *IF YOU MOVE ONTO YOUR OPPONENT'S CARDS, YOU MUST STOP AND FIGHT THEM.*

- ○ IF YOU MOVE ONTO AN OPPONENT'S CARD WHICH IS FACE DOWN, FLIP IT FACE UP BEFORE YOU FIGHT. (THE CARD STAYS FACE UP AFTER THE BATTLE.)

- ○ THERE ARE THREE OUTCOMES OF BATTLE:

  - ● *ONE CARD BEATS THE OTHER CARD.* REMOVE THE LOSING CARD FROM PLAY. THE WINNER DOESN'T GET TO TAKE IT. IF THE WINNING CARD MOVED ONTO THE LOSING CARD'S SPACE, THE WINNING CARD MUST STOP AND THE WINNING PLAYER'S TURN ENDS.

  - ● *BOTH CARDS DIE.* IF BOTH CARDS HAVE THE SAME SUIT, BOTH CARDS ARE REMOVED FROM PLAY.

  - ● *TIE.* BATTLES BETWEEN CERTAIN CARDS (LIKE HEARTS VERSUS DIAMONDS) RESULT IN A TIE. IN THIS CASE, THE PLAYER WHO STARTED THE BATTLE MUST MOVE THEIR CARD BACK TO ITS ORIGINAL POSITION AT THE START OF THE TURN. THAT PLAYER'S TURN ENDS.

WINNING THE GAME

- ○ TO WIN, YOU MUST ATTACK THE OTHER PLAYER'S JOKER, OR TRAP THEM SO THAT THEY CAN'T MOVE. (JOKERS CAN'T ATTACK OTHER CARDS, EXCEPT FOR ENEMY JOKERS.)

- ○ IF TWO JOKERS FIGHT EACH OTHER, THE ONE WHO INITIATED THE ATTACK WINS THE GAME.

THE RULES MIGHT SEEM COMPLICATED AT FIRST, BUT IT'S EASY ONCE YOU START PLAYING!!

MASTER OF THE CARDS

The "Duel Monsters" card game first appeared in volume two of the original **Yu-Gi-Oh!** graphic novel series. but it's in **Yu-Gi-Oh!: Duelist** (originally printed in Japan as volumes 8-31 of **Yu-Gi-Oh!**) that it gets really important. As many fans know, some of the card names are different between the English and Japanese versions. In case you play the game, or you're interested in playing, here's a rundown of the cards in this graphic novel. Some cards only appear in the **Yu-Gi-Oh!** video games, not in the actual collectible card game.

FIRST APPEARANCE IN THIS VOLUME	JAPANESE CARD NAME	ENGLISH CARD NAME
p.7	*Harpie Lady*	Harpy Lady
p.7	*Tiger Axe*	Tiger Axe
p. 9	*Mamono no Kariudo* (Demon Hunter)	Kojikocy
p.10	*Dengeki Muchi* (Electric Shock Whip)	Electro-Whip
p.11	Cyber Bondage	Cyber Bondage (NOTE: Not a real game card. Called "Cyber Shield" in the video games.)

GIANT SOLDIER OF STONE

[ROCK]
A giant statue made of stone. A punch from this creature has earth-shaking results.

ATK/1300 DEF/2000

JELLYFISH

[AQUA]
An almost invisible, semi-transparent jellyfish that drifts by the sea.

ATK/1200 DEF/1500

STOP DEFENSE

[MAGIC CARD]

Select 1 of your opponent's monsters and switch it to Attack Position. If the card is face-down, flip it face-up. If the card has a flip effect, it is activated immediately.

FIRST APPEARANCE IN THIS VOLUME	JAPANESE CARD NAME	ENGLISH CARD NAME
p.18	Baby Dragon	Baby Dragon
p.19	*Mangekyō: Karei naru Bunshin* (Kaleidoscope: Splendid Doppelganger)	Elegant Egotist
p.20	*Garoozis*	Garoozis
p.22	*Toki no Majutsushi* (Magician of Time)	Time Wizard
p.25	Thousand Dragon (NOTE: Japanese kanji reads: Thousand-year Dragon)	Thousand Dragon
p.44	Devil Kraken	Devil Kraken (NOTE: Not a real game card. Called "Fiend Kraken" in the video games.)
p.44	Imp	Imp (NOTE: Not a real game card. Called "Horned Imp" in the anime.)
p.51	Gremlin	Feral Imp

FIRST APPEARANCE IN THIS VOLUME	JAPANESE CARD NAME	ENGLISH CARD NAME
p.52	*Kurage Jellyfish* (Sea Moon Jellyfish)	Jellyfish
p.53	*Ikkakujû no Horn* (Unicorn's Horn)	Horn of the Unicorn
p.57	*Silver Fang*	Silver Fang
p.57	*Mashô no Tsuki* (Mystical Moon)	Mystical Moon
p.58	Leviathan (NOTE: Japanese text reads: Sea Dragon God)	Leviathan (NOTE: Not a real game card. Called "Kairyu-shin" (Sea Dragon God) in the video games.)
p.63	*Ganseki no Kyohei* (Giant Soldier of Stone)	Giant Soldier of Stone
p.63	Megalodon	Megalodon (NOTE: Not a real game card.)
p.68	*Curse of Dragon*	Curse of Dragon

HARPIE LADY

[WINGED BEAST]
This human-shaped animal with wings is beautiful to watch but deadly in battle.

ATK/1300 DEF/1400

ELECTRO-WHIP

[MAGIC CARD]

A Thunder-Type monster equipped with this card increases its Atk and Def by two points.

FERAL IMP

[FIEND]
A playful little fiend that lurks in the dark, waiting to attack an unwary enemy.

ATK/1300 DEF/1400

FIRST APPEARANCE IN THIS VOLUME	JAPANESE CARD NAME	ENGLISH CARD NAME
p.85	*Hitokui Shokubutsu* (Man-Eating Plant)	Man Eater (NOTE: Art looks different in the real card game.)
p.86	*Toride o Mamoru Yokuryû* (Fortress-Protecting Winged Dragon)	Winged Dragon, Guardian of the Fortress
p.86	Crocodilus	Crocodilus
p.87	*Elf no Senshi* (Elf Soldier)	Celtic Guardian
p.108	Minotaurus	Battle Ox
p.109	Black Magician	Dark Magician
p.110	Blue-Eyes White Dragon	Blue-Eyes White Dragon
p.120	*Shubi Fûji* (Defense Seal)	Stop Defense

FIRST APPEARANCE IN THIS VOLUME	JAPANESE CARD NAME	ENGLISH CARD NAME
p.124	Magical Silk Hat	Magical Hats
p.128	*Rokubôsei no Jubaku* (Binding Curse of the Hexagram)	Spellbinding Circle
p.141	Grappler	Grappler (NOTE: Not a real game card. Called "Grappler" in the video games.)
p.143	Holy Elf	Mystical Elf
p.147	*Sei naru Barrier Mirror Force* (Holy Barrier Mirror Force)	Mirror Force
p.148	*Kôgeki no Muryokuka* (Nullificiation of Attack)	Negate Attack
p.149	*Shisha Sosei* (Resurrection of the Dead)	Monster Reborn
p.179	*Nitô o Motsu King Rex* (Two-Headed King Rex)	Two-Headed King Rex

FIRST APPEARANCE IN THIS VOLUME	JAPANESE CARD NAME	ENGLISH CARD NAME
p.186	*Gyû Majin* (Ox Demon)	Battle Steer
p.187	Axe Raider	Axe Raider
p.188	Sword Dragon	Sword Dragon (NOTE: Not a real game card. Called "Sword Arm of Dragon" in the video games.)
p.190	*Gankutsu Majin Ogre Rock* (Grotto/Cave Golem/Djinn Ogre Rock)	Rock Ogre Grotto #1
p.192	*Megazaura*	Megasaurus (NOTE: Not a real game card. Called "Megazowler" in the video games.)
p.193	*Barbarian 2-Go* (Barbarian #2)	Swamp Battleguard
p.199	*Honô no Kenshi* (Swordsman of Flames)	Flame Swordsman

IN THE NEXT VOLUME...

The Flame Swordsman has turned the fight in Jonouchi's favor...but is it enough to beat Dinosaur Ryuzaki? Then, the diabolical Player Killer of Darkness, Pegasus's second gaming assassin, challenges Yugi to a duel in the dark! But across the ocean in Japan, an even greater gaming force has been awakened. Kaiba, Yugi's No. 1 rival, is back. Back to reclaim his fortune...back to get revenge on Pegasus...and back to defeat Yugi and his friends!

COMING APRIL 2006!

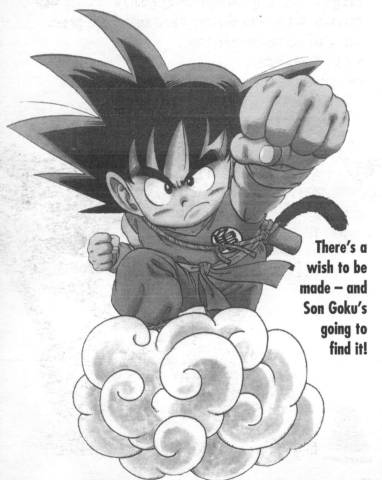

DRAG☆N BALL

™

There's a wish to be made — and Son Goku's going to find it!

THE ULTIMATE SWORDSMAN HAS COME
TO GOLLANCZ

Rurouni
Kenshin™

There is a legend of a wandering
swordsman. Unmatched in skill,
powerful, mysterious — and lost to
the world for over a decade.
Or so they thought.

ONAMI

Yu-Gi-Oh!
TRADING CARD GAME
COLLECTIBLE TINS

HE ESSENTIAL DUELLIST ELEMENTS

ommand the duel with these essential Yu-Gi-Oh! TCG COLLECTOR TINS!

Play out the power struggle between the elements with the full set of 2005 limited edition tins. These tins are made to fit your duelling deck and are fully charged with the hottest monster cards yet! Each tin contains one of these limited edition monster cards (Gilford the Lightning, Vorse Raider, Dark Magician Girl, Rocket Warrior, Exarion Universe, Panther Warrior) and 5 booster packs. There are 6 tins in all, so choose your weapon and alter the structure of duelling!

www.yugioh-card.com

COMPLETE OUR SURVEY AND
LET US KNOW WHAT YOU THINK!

❑ Please do NOT send me information about Gollancz Manga, or other Orion titles, products, news and events, special offers or other information.

Name: _____

Address: _____

Town: _____ County: _____ Postcode: _____

❑ Male ❑ Female   Date of Birth (dd/mm/yyyy): ___/___/_____
                  (under 13? Parental consent required)

What race/ethnicity do you consider yourself? (please check one)

❑ Asian   ❑ Black   ❑ Hispanic

❑ White/Caucasian   ❑ Other: _____

Which Gollancz Manga series did you purchase?

❑ Case Closed   ❑ Dragon Ball   ❑ Flame of Recca   ❑ Fushigi Yûgi
❑ Maison Ikkoku ❑ One Piece   ❑ Rurouni Kenshin   ❑ Yu-Gi-Oh!
❑ Yu-Gi-Oh! Duelist

What other Gollancz Manga series have you tried?

❑ Case Closed   ❑ Dragon Ball   ❑ Flame of Recca   ❑ Fushigi Yûgi
❑ Maison Ikkoku ❑ One Piece   ❑ Rurouni Kenshin   ❑ Yu-Gi-Oh!
❑ Yu-Gi-Oh! Duelist

How many anime and/or manga titles have you purchased in the last year?
How many were Gollancz Manga titles?

Anime	Manga	GM
❑ None	❑ None	❑ None
❑ 1-4	❑ 1-4	❑ 1-4
❑ 5-10	❑ 5-10	❑ 5-10
❑ 11+	❑ 11+	❑ 11+

Reason for purchase: (check all that apply)

❑ Special Offer ❑ Favourite title ❑ Gift
❑ In store promotion If so please indicate which store: _____
❑ Recommendation ❑ Other_____

Where did you make your purchase?

❑ Bookshop ❑ Comic Shop ❑ Music Store
❑ Newsagent ❑ Video Game Store ❑ Supermarket
❑ Other: _____ ❑ Online:_____

What kind of manga would you like to read?

❑ Adventure ❑ Comic Strip ❑ Fantasy
❑ Fighting ❑ Horror ❑ Mystery
❑ Romance ❑ Science Fiction ❑ Sports
❑ Other:_____

Which do you prefer?

❑ Sound effects in English
❑ Sound effects in Japanese with English captions
❑ Sound effects in Japanese only with a glossary at the back

Want to find out more about Manga?

Look it up at www.orionbooks.co.uk, or www.viz.com

THANK YOU!

Please send the completed form to:

Manga Survey
Orion Books
Orion House
5 Upper St Martin's Lane
London, WC2H 9EA